THE NEW MILLENNIUM COLLECTION

SPAIN

MASTERPIECES OF ART AND NATURE, TREASURES OF CULTURE
AND TRADITION, IN THE LAND OF BULLFIGHTING AND FLAMENCO DANCING,
WHERE EVERYTHING ECHOES OF SUN AND PASSION

BONECHI

SUMMARY

HISTORICAL NOTES

With its shores swept by the cold waters of the Atlantic Ocean on one coast and by the warmer waters of the Mediterranean Sea on the other (resulting in a variety of climates ranging from cool continental air on the inland plateaux to intense heat in the southern regions), Spain covers a great part of the Iberian Peninsula, flanked by Portugal. Its fertile soil, its wealth of underground mineral resources, the abundance of fish in its seas and its typical, pleasant scenery have all contributed over the centuries to making this land a much sought after place for many populations. Man started living here at around 800,000 BC; the first inhabitants were groups of hunters, followed many years later by tribes of sheep-farmers and, around the year 5000 BC, by agriculture farmers. Later on, colonisers from farther afield arrived, creating not only colonies here, but also bringing their own particular forms of culture with them: the first to land on the Spanish shores were the Phoenicians, around 1100 BC, who founded prosperous settlements particularly along the South-East coastline; the Greeks were the next to arrive, coming here in the VII century and settling along the North-East coast of the country; the last to land in the peninsula were the Carthaginians who came in 228 BC and began their surge of conquests in Andalusia. However, these highly evolved 'foreigners', who intended transforming Spain into one of their colonies, soon found themselves facing the native inhabitants and resident cultures: like the powerful Tartessian Kingdom, which appeared in the southern part of Spain in the VIII century BC and which was conquered by Hamilcar Barca's strong Carthaginian army only at the end of the III century BC; or the tough, bellicose Celtiberians, who were a mixed-blood race generated from native tribes and the Celts who had come down from the North many years previously to conquer the Spanish plateaux. It was these Celtiberians and the Carthaginian troops of Hamilcar's son, Hannibal, that Scipio Africanus had

to face when he landed at Emporium (now Empúries, on the North-East coast of Spain) in 218 BC, giving rise to the Second Punic War and the Roman conquest of the peninsula. However, while the Carthaginians were completely overcome by 206 BC, conquering the rest of the country that was so fiercely defended by the local people proved to be a much more arduous task, so much so that Augustus was able to proclaim the conquest completed only in 19 BC. In 74 AD, Vespasian granted Roman citizenship to all the cities in the country, and for centuries thereafter Spain was the granary of the Roman Empire, thanks to the vast areas where cereals were extensively grown, and it became one of its principal sources of minerals. However, Spain also produced many famous people for Rome, from the Emperor Trajan to Seneca, the philosopher, and in return the cities were extended and embellished, facilities (roads, aqueducts etc.) were created, new centres were founded and majestic monuments were erected. Nevertheless, when Roman supremacy began to decline, Spain, which was a peripheral part of the Empire, was one of the first provinces to pay the consequences: halfway through the III century there had been already numerous incursions by the Franks coming down from the

Charles V in a XVII century painting by the Anthony van Dyck School.

North, but the finishing blow came from the Vandals, Swabians and Alanians, who crossed over the Pyrenees in 409 and ransacked the peninsula. It was the Visigoths, another Germanic tribe, who took over from the Romans after conquering the peninsula in 415: once they had established their court at Barcelona they left the political, juridical and administrative structures created by the Romans practically untouched, imposing only their supremacy supported by a solid military regime. On the other hand, they tried in vain to force Aryanism on a country where Christianity had been spreading since the III century: as a matter of fact, the Visigoth King Recaredo actually converted to the Roman Catholic Church at the end of the VI century and

3

became the first Christian sovereign of Spain; he promoted the first serious contacts between the Hispanic people and their former invaders, thus leading the way to unification of the rich Hispanic-Roman culture with the rougher, more uncouth culture imported by the Visigoths. By the VII century, however, the strength of the Visigoth kingdom in Spain began to decline, undermined by the internal disputes that tormented the aristocratic ranks: in this situation they were unable to ward off the advancing Arabs and Berbers, who landed on the southern coasts of the country in 711. These very quickly conquered the whole of Spain, except for a small strip of land in the Asturias mountains where the Moors – as the Muslim invaders were soon called – were opposed by a large group of Christians and Visigoth noblemen: the victory of the Visigoths over the Arabs at Cavadonga in 722 was considered a message from Heaven and was actually the first step towards the future, heroic Reconquista of Christianity in the whole country. In the meantime, however, the Moors, frustrated by the ambitious project of subjecting the continent after the defeat suffered by Carlo Martello's troops at Poitiers in 732, dedicated themselves to reorganising the Spanish territories they had already conquered and which they collectively called Al Andalus: this gave birth to the powerful caliphate of Cordoba and a rich, refined culture began to flourish, one that was to reach heights of splendour unrivalled elsewhere in Europe and destined to leave indelible traces in Spanish history. Moorish Spain asserted itself as a mighty power, to the forefront in all branches of knowledge, from mathematics to architecture, from astronomy to decorative arts, from warfare to navigation techniques. Meanwhile, Christian resistance was becoming organised in the northern parts of the Iberian Peninsula: in 744, Alphonse I of Asturias was very successful in León, occupying part of Galicia and Cantabria; in the IX century, Alphonse II established the capital of the new Christian kingdom in Oviedo, forming an alliance with the Basques who had always been proud of their independence and were obstinate opponents of the Moors; in 905 it was the turn of Navarra to become a Christian realm under Sancho I, whereas García I transferred the capital of the Asturian kingdom from Oviedo to León in 913. In 976, though, when rule in Cordoba was taken over by Al-Mansur, a strong-willed military dictator, all the internal struggles that had weakened Moorish domination were appeased and Arabian vengeance fell upon the Christian kingdoms: Barcelona was set on fire and its inhabitants were either killed or captured, while devastating raids upset Asturias and Catalonia, Navarra and León, Aragona and even Santiago de Compostela, where the Cathedral was completely destroyed; only the doors and bells were saved, but they were taken to Cordoba and used for making ceilings and lamps in the Great Mosque that was being built there. However, on the death of Al Mansur in 1002, the situation was not long in changing: aided by the disintegration of the Arabian State that was breaking up into small independent kingdoms, the taifas that were devoted to secessionism, the Christians advanced compact towards the South and while the Count of Barcelona marched towards Cordoba, Sancho III the Great, King of Navarra, was acknowledged sovereign of Aragona and Castile, as well as of the city of León. From then on, everything seemed fated: in 1013 the Caliphate of Cordoba fell at last, in 1037 Ferdinand I united León and Castile under the one crown, in 1085 Alphonse VI of Castile re-conquered Toledo, in 1094 El Cid overcame Valencia, while the marriage performed in the middle of the XII century between the Count of Barcelona, Ramón Berengario IV and Petronila, daughter of the King of Aragona, led to the unification of Aragona and Catalonia under the rule of their

Henry of Navarra, crowned Henry IV of France, depicted at the Battle of Ivry in a painting by Rubens.

Charles IV and his large family in an official portrait by Goya.
Below: the portrait of Philip II by Alonso Sánchez Coello.

son, Alphonse II. In the meantime, the Almohads, a Berber tribe that had come over from Morocco, landed in Spain and joined another North African tribe, the Almoravids, who, in spite of their decline, still kept vast possessions in the South of the peninsula. These Almohads invaded Andalusia in 1195, forcefully driving out thousands of Mozarabi (Christians who had continued to live and work in Saracen territory) and establishing their capital in Seville. But the reaction of the Christian world was quick and determined: Pope Innocence III proclaimed a crusade and in 1212, at Las Navas de Tolosa, the combined armadas under Alphonse VIII of Castile, Pedro II of Aragona and Sancho VII of Navarra overthrew the Almohad armies. Therefore, while James I conquered Valencia and the Balearic Islands, Ferdinand III united Castile and León under his crown (1230). And six years after, Cordoba surrendered to this king. Nevertheless, there were still many places in the hands of the Muslims – so many, in fact, that from then on the Reconquista proceeded at a gradual pace, performing one small step after another: in 1246, Ferdinand III conquered Jaén, in 1248 Seville fell, whereas Granada and Malaga became part of a new Muslim state protected by the Christians, under the Arabian Nasiridi dynasty which offered asylum to thousands of fleeing Moors. The fact that so many different Christian monarchs reigned in Spain, all inevitably divided by rivalry and dispute, was not exactly an advantage for the final Reconquista: this is why it could not be considered completed until all the different crowns had become united. This took place in 1469 when Ferdinand, King of Aragona, Valencia and Catalonia, married Isabella, Queen of Castile, Murcia and Almería. In effect, once the feudal system had been abolished and the solidity of a sole monarchy had been established, the 'Catholic Monarchs' gave the country a new configuration: through Pope Sixtus IV they introduced the Inquisition in 1478, then in 1492, the same year as the fall of Granada (which was the final act of unification in Spain), they ordered the expulsion of all Jews and proceeded, in 1502, to banish all the Moors who had not converted to the Catholic Church. However, 1492 was also the year when America was discovered by Christopher Columbus, whose caravels

5

sailed under the Spanish Royal flag: conquering these new, immense territories (after landing in the Caribbean Islands, the Conquistadores reached the continent where they occupied Mexico in 1519, Peru in 1532 then Chile in 1541) meant the importation of enormous quantities of products and resources that were fundamental for the future of the Spanish kingdom. Furthermore, navigation and shipping was greatly stimulated and Seville became one of the most important ports in Europe while, over and above all the gold, silver and precious stones that were brought into Spain, new products were introduced, like potatoes, maize, tobacco and cocoa. Nevertheless, there was also a dark side to this moment of great splendour: while the converted Moors in the country began protesting vehemently against persecutions and unjust taxes, outside of Spain much clamour was manifested against the extermination of the American natives. And though Charles I, grandson of the Catholic Monarchs and Emperor of the Holy Roman Empire as Charles V (since he was also heir to the Hapsburgs) had led the Spanish troops into battlefields all over Europe, Philip II, his son and successor to the dominions of Spain, Flanders and Italy, while being a competent administrator was faced with a kingdom that was only apparently opulent since it was on the verge of financial ruin because of the many wars that had been fought; and in 1588, Philip witnessed the destruction of the famous Invincible Armada, the feared naval fleet that had set forth in vain to conquer England. The powers of Spain and its monarchy in Europe began to decline from this sad event onwards: in fact, though the monarchs did much for fostering the arts and sciences all through the XVII century, embellishing and enriching cities and buildings as well as founding the Siglo de Oro for art and literature (Cervantes, Lope de Vega and El Greco are but examples), they also involved the country in exhausting wars in the Netherlands and in Italy without taking into account either the financial difficulties of the country or its practically drained economy, since agriculture was undergoing a period of critical recession, foreign debt was astronomical and

industry was completely neglected. Worn out by many years of conflict with France, the last of the Hapsburgs in Spain, Charles II, died heirless in 1700, leaving the crown to Philip of Anjou, the future Philip V and grandson of Louis XIV, the Sun King. This created much anger among the Austrians who, fearing that France would consequently have excessive power, opposed it by appointing another pretender to the throne, Archduke Charles, to whom Catalonia, Valencia and the Balearic Islands swore their loyalty. This led to the lengthy, arduous War of Succession (1702-1714) which ended when Philip V was acknowledged the rightful king without, however, Flanders, Italy and Minorca, and losing Gibraltar which became English (Treaties of Utrecht). This first Bourbon king – just like those who came after him – had precise targets in mind: a stronger State with less powers to the Church, revival of the economy of the land by first of all invigorating its industries, reorganisation of military spheres and incentivation of the arts and culture. His successor, Charles III (1759-1788), was also very actively involved in this difficult task of restoring the spirit and substance of Spain, and though a fervent Catholic he resolutely expelled the General Inquisitor from the land and then, in 1766, the Jesuits. The Royal Palace in Madrid was completed thanks to him, and the Prado Museum and reorganisation of both the river system and network of roads throughout the country were other important features in the programme he carried out; moreover, he was also responsible for the progressive aperture of Spain towards the new philosophy that drifted in from France in the wake of the Enlightenment Movement. Charles IV proved to have a completely different personality since he was first of all a victim of his despotic wife, Maria Luisa of Parma, and tormented by Napoleon who was already strongly present in the country and who convinced him in 1808 to banish his rebel son, Ferdinand, and to abdicate in favour of Bonaparte's brother, Joseph. Spain, however, already humiliated by the defeat of its fleet, which had been practically annihilated by Nelson in the Battle of Trafalgar in 1805, reacted vehemently: the peasants were the first to revolt and insurrection gradually extended to all the regions, causing the War of Independence that con-

Picturesque and significant illustrations depicting one of the worst events in Spanish history: the ferocious Inquisition.

The modern, popular and much loved Spanish Royal Family:
King Juan Carlos de Bourbon and Queen Sophia of Greece, above with their
three children by their sides – Felipe, heir to the throne and Prince of Asturias,
Cristina and Elena.

tinued until the fall of Napoleon in 1814. Just before this, in 1812, the Spanish Court met in Cadiz and proclaimed the country's first liberal Constitution. However, the Spanish Restoration soon met with the determination of Ferdinand VII who, having refused to acknowledge this Constitution, established rigid absolutism in the country and reinstated both the Inquisition and the Jesuits once more, as well as opposing all initiatives. Nevertheless, while on one hand the king's intemperate and repressive conservatism first caused the revolt and then the secession of the American colonies, on the other hand his late marriage to the liberal Maria Cristina de Bourbon of Sicily and his decision to change the laws of royal succession in favour of his daughter Isabella, engendered the wrath of the conservative extremists in Spain, who responded by counterattacking him with his brother, Don Carlos: hence, in 1833 the so-called Carlist Wars commenced and resulted in many decades of violent civil conflicts between liberals and conservatives supported by the Church, with some particularly ferocious episodes; there was an interval in 1873 when the First Republic took place, but schism within Spanish society was serious and lasted until the end of the XIX century when Alphonse XII brought the conflicts onto a purely political plane. Therefore, at the dawn of the XX century, in a country that was substantially declining, the few cautious attempts at recovering its economy and finances were insufficient for keeping at bay the discontent that rippled through Spain and that expanded after the loss of Cuba and the Philippines (1898). In spite of the flourishing revival of the arts and culture, the continual bloodshed caused by the anarchists, the revolt of the workers, the disastrous results of warfare in Morocco and the brutal repression of

the protests which followed, merely exasperated the people even more. This led to a convulsive series of events: strikes and public demonstrations kindled by anarchist and socialist workers' unions; order reinstated by the resolute dictatorship of Miguel Primo de Rivera (1923), which did not survive the 1929 great depression, however; the 1931 elections, won by the left-wing, which resulted in the removal of Alphonse XIII – on the throne since 1902 – and the proclamation of the Second Republic; the increasingly fierce conflicts between Right and Left wings that led to the outbreak of a terrible Civil War on 18th July 1936; after three years of fighting and bloodshed, the victory of General Francisco Franco's Nationalists openly backed, not only by the Spanish Army, but also by Italy and Germany; the consequent slaughter of thousands of supporters of the republican movement, many of whom were well-known intellectuals; the substantially neutral bearing kept during World War II except for the support the new dictator offered the German-Italian alliance; the Francoist regime, (backed by both the Church and the Military and only initially contrasted by NATO and the United Nations), with its policy of progressive recovery of Spanish economy, sagacious social politics and particular attention focused on the diffusion of culture; and, lastly, when Franco died in 1975 and one the Bourbon heirs, Juan Carlos, grandson of Alphonse XIII, sat once more on the throne. Under this new, farsighted sovereign with clearly liberal ideas, Spain has marched along the road to democracy with determination and speed, establishing itself in the Europe of the Third Millennium, not only as a modern and economically sound nation, but also as a land that has experienced a civil, political, social and intellectual awakening.

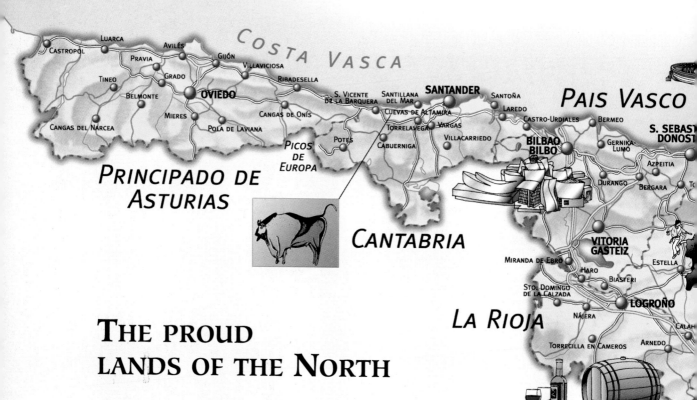

THE PROUD LANDS OF THE NORTH

The Atlantic Ocean, the Pyrenees and the Mediterranean Sea demarcate the northern and eastern parts of North Spain, where a succession of green hills covered with vine-yards can be found next to sandy or rocky beaches on the shores of bays and in-lets, which harbour both tiny ports and large cities, and where high snow-capped peaks tower over deep valleys dug out by long rivers. Proud and tough lands, just like their inhabitants; people who have come to be particularly jealous of their identity, their traditions and their own language as a result of hundreds of years of distinguished history and lengthy independence. From Catalonia to Aragona, from Navarra to the Basque Counties, from Cantabria to La Rioja, and to Asturias: Spain is also these individual, distinct realities. Moreover, the severe-looking mediaeval villages,

the hard-working inhabitants, the unimpaired vitality of the forests, as well as the outstanding and particular style of the various artistic items produced, are all demonstrations that even Time will find it difficult to change the harsh, strong fascination of Northern Spain.

FRANCIA

COMUNIDAD
FORAL DE
NAVARRA

PIRINEOS

VIELHA   CATALUNYA

ANDORRA

RONCESVALLES

URGUETE
FZIN

AOIZ

MPLONA
IRUÑA

LEYRE

SOS DEL REY CATÓLICO   JACA

OLITE

BOLTAÑA

PONT DE SUERT   SORT   LA SEU D'URGELL   PUIGCERDÀ   PORTBOU

MOLLÓ

TUDELA

EJEA DE LOS
CABALLEROS   HUESCA   TREMP   ORGANYÀ   BAGÀ   RIBES DE FRESER   FIGUERES

ISONA   RIPOLL   BESALÚ   ROSES

BORJA   OLOT

BERGA   GIRONA   LA BISBAL
D'EMPORDÀ

TAMARITE DE LITERA   SOLSONA   VIC

CARDONA   STA. COLOMA DE FARNERS   LLAGOSTERA   PALAMÓS

ZARAGOZA   SARIÑENA   BALAGUER   ST. FELIU DE GUÍXOLS

MANRESA   TOSSA DE MAR

CERVERA   GRANOLLERS   ARENYS DE MAR

FRAGA   LLEIDA   TERRASSA

PINA   LES BORGES
BLANQUES   IGUALADA   SABADELL   MATARÓ

BUJARALOZ   BADALONA

ALATAYUD   ST. FELIU DE
LLOBREGAT   BARCELONA

VILAFRANCA
DEL PENEDÈS

OCA   VALLS   EL VENDRELL   SITGES

CASPE   FALSET   REUS   VILANOVA
I LA GELTRÚ

CALAMOCHA   ALCAÑIZ   GANDESA

MONTALBÁN   ALCORISA   VALDERROBRES   TARRAGONA   L'HOSPITÁLET DE L'INFANT

CASTELLOTE   TORTOSA   L'AMETLLA DE MAR

ALIAGA

BARRACÍN

TERUEL   ST. CARLES DE LA RÀPITA

COSTA BRAVA

COSTA DORADA

R. Ebro

MAR MEDITERRÁNEO

N

BARCELONA

Barcelona, the vivacious chief city of Catalonia, is unique in the world: for centuries the traditional pride of its people, closely bound to its roots, has merged with the typical cosmopolitan life-style of all great commercial ports, and traces of past splendour and thousands of years of history live in harmony next to amazing creations, generated from the fervid imagination of much more modern artists, and to imposing monuments erected at the dawn of the Third Millennium. This is probably due, in part, to the acquisition of long-standing independence in the whole region; however, this city in particular, with its name reminiscent of Hamilcar Barca, the Carthaginian warrior, achieved its position in the Middle Ages and obstinately maintained it, first as a prominent and very busy centre for trading and banking (one of the most important in the continent) and later, after the discovery of America, as

one of the leading industrial cities in Europe. In effect, the three main districts in the city still reflect the different and very distinct spirits of Barcelona. The **Old City** (*Ciutat Vella* in Catalan, the local dialect with all the dignity of a actual language), one of the largest and best-preserved historical centres in the world, still bears intact its charming, mediaeval appearance. The **Gothic District** (*Barri Gòtic*) is the oldest part and contains some of the city's most important historical buildings: here one finds the sombre **Royal Palace** (*Palau Reial Major*), seat of the powerful Counts of Barcelona from the XIII century onwards, with its XIV century *Capella Reial de Santa Ágata* and the *Saló del Tinell* of the same period, a vast Gothic hall where the Catholic Monarchs, Ferdinand and Isabella, welcomed Christopher Columbus on his return from his first, successful voyage to the West Indies, and where the Inquisition held its court at a later date; the **Palau de la Generalitat** where the Catalonia parliament meets, a building with austere Gothic interiors and a Renaissance façade displaying a

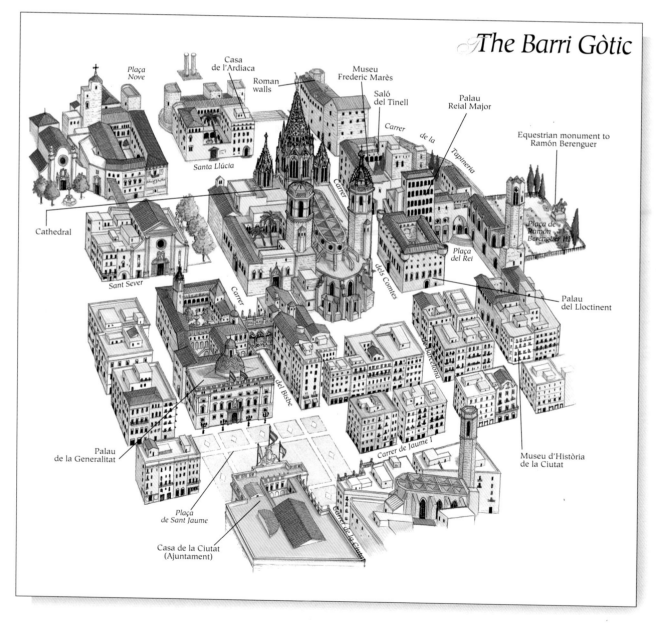

The Barri Gòtic

Plaça Nove

Casa de l'Ardiaca

Roman walls

Museu Frederic Marès

Saló del Tinell

Palau Reial Major

Carrer de la Tapineria

Equestrian monument to Ramón Berenguer

Santa Llúcia

Carrer

Plaça de Ramón Berenguer III

Cathedral

Plaça del Rei

Sant Sever

Carrer

dels Comtes

Palau del Lloctinent

del Bisbe

Carrer de Jaume I

Barcelona

Museu d'Història de la Ciutat

Palau de la Generalitat

Plaça de Sant Jaume

Carrer de la Ciutat

Casa de la Ciutat (Ajuntament)

statue of St. George (*Sant Jordi*), the Patron Saint of the region; the **Casa de la Ciutat**, the XIV Municipal building where the Council (the government assembly) held its sessions in the picturesque, monumental *Saló de Cent* (XV century), so-called because of the number (100) of members in the assembly. The elaborate Gothic spires of the splendid **Cathedral** stand out in the middle of this district: built over a Roman temple that was substituted in the IV century by an Early-Christian basilica, later dedicated to St. Eulalia (the martyr and Patron Saint of Barcelona, buried in the crypt) and destroyed by the Moors in 985, it was subsequently rebuilt in Romanesque style half way through the XI century. The Cathedral as we see it today was started in 1298 and while its appearance is undoubtedly Gothic it still preserves certain Romanesque elements, like the

The spectacular façade of Barcelona Cathedral, which was not finished until 1889 in the soaring Gothic style foreseen in the designs drawn up in 1408 by Charles Galters, the French architect.
The imposing central spire was completed in 1913.

pre-existent *Capella de Santa Llúcia* (mid-XIII century) and the twin octagonal-base *towers*. The façade, though designed by the architect Charles Galters in 1408, was not finished until 1889 and the central spire was not completed until 1913. The *interiors* are magnificent, with a Catalan Gothic *nave* surrounded by 28 chapels along the sides, and figured *Choir-stalls* behind a XVI century marble enclosure. Even the green and pleasant Gothic

Cloisters deserve a visit to admire the fountain and enjoy the fragrances of the orange trees and magnolias, and also the *Vestry Museum* with its small but invaluable collection of religious objects, paraments and works of art.

Opposite the imposing façade of the Cathedral stands the picturesque *Casa de l'Ardiaca*, the Archdeacon's residence, erected in the XII century next to the ancient Roman walls and the Bishop's

Gate. Reconstructed at various stages between the XVI and XVIII centuries, it now boasts a pleasant patio surrounded by a colonnade that calls to mind the peaceful atmosphere of Moorish gardens. However, many of the beautiful antique buildings in the Barri Gòtic district, all accurately and sometimes specifically restored, have become the seats of modern institutions that are nevertheless strictly connected to the roots and traditions so dear to Barcelona and its inhabitants. For example, the *Museu Frederic Marès* that occupies some of the rooms in the enormous antique Royal Palace. This famous sculptor, traveller and collector lived here for several years and in 1948 he opened his museum in it to display, besides his vast collections of Romanesque and Gothic religious art, all different types of collections, from clocks to toys and from cloths to cameras, which give an idea of the variety of fields that had captured the interest of this creative artist, who died almost 100 years old in 1991.

A XIV Gothic-style residence was literally dismantled, removed and rebuilt on its present site in 1931 to hold the interesting **Museu d'Història de la Ciutat**, a special institution that documents the historical-architectural development of Barcelona, starting from the remains of the walled Roman settlement and going right through the rapid urban development that distinguished the golden ages, the XIII, XIV and XIV centuries. An unexpected treasure came to light during the reconstruction of the building: the excavations required to support the building revealed large sections of ancient Roman structures (aqueducts, roads, sewers, baths, floors and paving), while parts of the walls of the same period were linked up with the new building. Very interesting material from different periods in history, from bas-relief sculptures to statues, from objects used for worship to elements from important constructions in the city, are all displayed on various floors of the museum.

A few examples of priceless antique works of art kept in the Museu d'Història de la Ciutat (above) and in the Museu Marès.

The Picasso Museum: a painting belonging to the Las Meniñas *series (1957) and* Harlequin *from the Blue Period, two of Picasso's most famous masterpieces.*

Once out of the mediaeval surroundings of the Gothic District and through the Old City towards the port, visitors come across one of the other institutions Barcelona is famous for, and rightly proud of. This is the great museum dedicated to Pablo Picasso, who came to the city as a youth in 1895 to join his father; his first works were produced here and were the result of the stimulation Picasso received from the eclectic and extremely creative atmosphere that reigned, and from the cultural awakening that invaded the streets and captured the spirit of the intellectuals at that time. The **Picasso Museum** was opened in 1963 and occupies three buildings, all mediaeval constructions: the *Palau Berenguer de Anguilar*, the *Palau Baró de Castellet* and the *Palau Meca*. The first pieces in the collection were donated by Jaime Sabartes, one of Picasso's friends and admirers who owned many of the artist's works. Following this, Picasso himself greatly increased the collection, then other pieces purchased later on by the Museum now make a total of approximately 3,000 works on view, divided into three sections: drawing and paintings (some of which are the ones he produced as an adolescent in Barcelona), etchings and prints, ceramics.

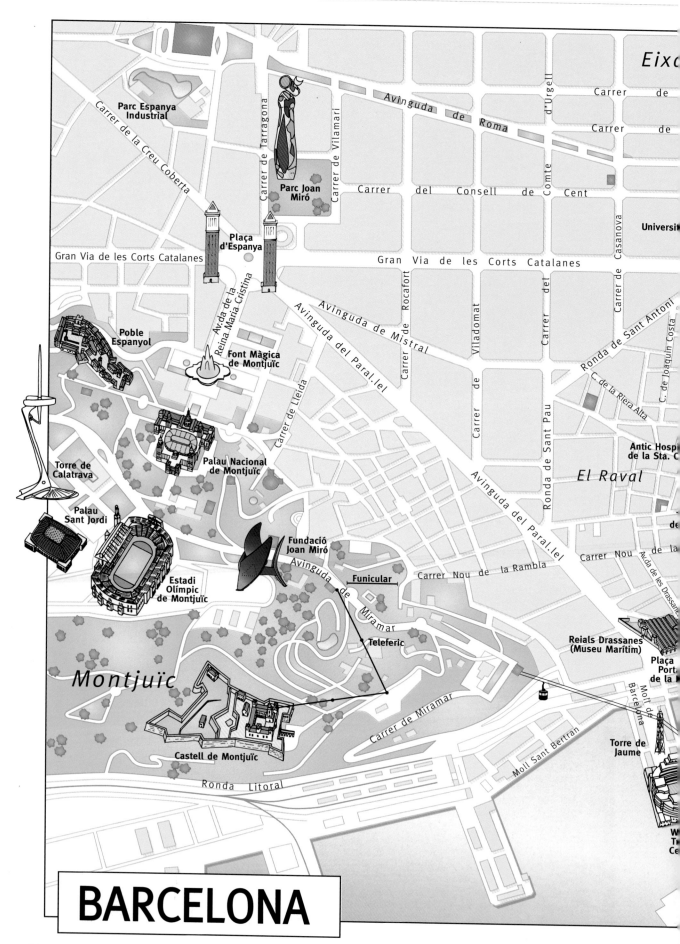

Eix

Carrer de

Avinguda de Roma

Carrer de

Universi

Parc Espanya Industrial

Carrer de la Creu Coberta

Carrer de Tarragona

Carrer de Vilamari

Carrer del Consell de Cent

Comte d'Urgell

Parc Joan Miró

Plaça d'Espanya

Gran Via de les Corts Catalanes

Gran Via de les Corts Catalanes

Carrer de Rocafort

Carrer de Viladomat

Carrer de

Carrer del

Carrer de Casanova

Av.da de la Reina Maria Cristina

Avinguda de Mistral

Avinguda del Paral.lel

Ronda de Sant Antoni

C. de Joaquín Costa

Poble Espanyol

Font Màgica de Montjuïc

Carrer de Lleida

Carrer de Sant Pau

C. de la Riera Alta

Antic Hosp de la Sta. C

El Raval

Torre de Calatrava

Palau Nacional de Montjuïc

Avinguda del Paral.lel

Palau Sant Jordi

Fundació Joan Miró

Avinguda de Miramar

Carrer Nou de la Rambla

Carrer Nou de la Rambla

de

Av.da de les Drassanes

Estadi Olímpic de Montjuïc

Funicular

Teleferic

Reials Drassanes (Museu Marítim)

Plaça Port de la

Montjuïc

Carrer de Miramar

Moll de Barcelona

Castell de Montjuïc

Moll Sant Bertran

Torre de Jaume

Ronda Litoral

W Tr Ce

BARCELONA

Casa
"Les Punxes"

Casa Milá
"La Pedrera"

Avinguda Diagonal

Carrer de Mallorca

Plaça de la
Sagrada
Familia

Sagrada
Familia

Carrer de Mallorca

llorca

Carrer de Mallorca

Casa
Batlló

Fundació
Antoni
Tàpies

Carrer de Valencia

Carrer de Valencia

encia

Avinguda Diagonal

Carrer d' Aragó

Casa
Amatller

Casa Lleó
Morera

rrer del Consell de Cent

Carrer del Consell de Cent

Passeig de Gràcia

de Roger Llúria

de Girona

Passeig de Sant Joan

Plaça de
Braus
Monumental

Gran Via de les Corts Catalanes

Plaça de
Tetuan

Gran Via de les Corts Catalanes

de la
sitat

Ronda de la Universitat

Ronda de la Universitat

Carrer de Nàpols

Carrer de la Marina

seu d'Art
temporani
Barcelona
(MACBA)

Plaça de
Catalunya

Ronda

Via Laietana

de

Sant Pere

Carrer de Ribes

de Ribes

Carrer de la Marina

e
els

La Rambla

Barri
Gòtic

Palau
de la Música
Catalana

Arc de Triomf

Parc Estació
del Nord

Avinguda Meridiana

queria

Palau de
la Virreina

Catedral

Plaça
Antoni
Maura

La Ribera

Carrer de Comerç

Santa
Maria
del Pi

Palau
de la
Generalitat

Plaça de
Sant Jaume

C. de la Princesa

Passeig de Pujades

u

C. de Ferran

Plaça
Reial

Ciutat
Vella

Via Laietana

Sta. Maria
del Mar

Parc de la
Ciutadella

Carrer de Wellington

Ramon Turró

Carrer de la Marina

Vila
Olímpica

Plaça
d'Antoni Lopez

Parc
Zoològic

Passeig de Colom

Estació
de França

Passeig de Circumval.lacio

Avinguda d' Icaria

Ronda Litoral

Palau de Mar
(Museu d'Història
de Catalunya)

Passeig Joan de Borbó

PORT
OLÍMPIC

Port Vell

Barceloneta

Platja Barceloneta

Torre de
Sant Sebastià

Platja de Sant Sebastià

MAR MEDITERRÀNIA

N

LAS RAMBLAS

We are still in the heart of the Old City, here, yet the atmosphere feels suddenly different when, just South-West of the Barri Gòtic, the almost two-Km long pedestrian street, the **Ramblas**, appears: an elegant tree-lined avenue milling with people at all hours of the day – and night. This is a series of streets called *Les Rambles* in Catalan dialect (*Rambla dels Canaletes, Rambla dels Estudis, Rambla de Sant Josep or de las Flors, Rambla dels Caputxins* or *del Centre, Rambla de Santa Monica*, which extend one after another in a direct line from *Plaça de Catalunya* to *Plaça del Portal de la Pau*) and all full of kiosks, stalls, flower-vendors, picturesque cafés, street artists, musicians and jugglers, and a host of vendors and people of all different types. These Ramblas cover the course of what was the bed of a river (*ramla* in Arab), a seasonal torrent that used to run outside the XIII walls of Barcelona creating a sort of ditch, which was then covered in. On the banks of these *Ramblas* and in their immediate surroundings, where convents, monasteries and even a university (no longer in existence) once stood for centuries when the torrent was still subject to seasonal swelling, there are now many magnificent buildings that give this important thoroughfare an elegant and versatile appearance: from the **Reial Acadèmia de Cièncias i Arts**, subsequently transformed into a theatre, to the XVIII century **Palau Moja**; from the **Palau de la Virreina** that owes its name to the fact that in 1777 it accommodated the wife of the Spanish Viceroy in Peru, who had it built and embellished with fine statues, to the **Boquería**, the most famous and liveliest food market in the city (also known as the *Mercat de Sant Josep* and held under an enormous structure made of iron); from the **Gran Teatre del Liceu**, the XIX Barcelona Opera House that has been gutted by fire many times, to the **Museu de Cera**, a curious XIX institution where hundreds of valuable pieces are displayed. Even the squares that open out here and there along the various *Ramblas* are full of elegant, architectural features: for example, the splendid **Plaça de la Boquería**, with its brightly coloured mosaic paving made by Miró in his unmistakable style in 1976; or the spacious New-classical **Plaça Reial**, erected in mid-XIX century and graced not only by a fine arcade but also by the presence of palm trees and elegant *lamps* designed by Gaudí.

However, there are many places that have become traditional meeting points for both the inhabitants of Barcelona and tourists: from the *Font dels Canaletes*, a delicate iron fountain made in the XIX century, to the famous *Café Zurich* on *Rambla dels Canaletes*, to the popular *Café de l'Opera*. Not far from the **Old Port** (*Port Vell*) where the *Ramblas* finally end in the *Plaça del Portal de la Pau*, stands the **monument to Christopher Columbus** (who landed here in 1493 on his return from his first voyage to America), one of the most famous statues in Barcelona, designed by Gaietà Buigas in 1888 for the Universal Exhibition. This stunning statue, made by Rafael Arché, is poised on a 60-metre high iron column that holds a lift inside the shaft for carrying visitors up to the platform at the top. Colombo's stretched-out arm points to the old, covered **docks** (*Drassanes*) that are now dry but which were once the site of famous and very busy shipyards; now they hold the well-appointed **Museu Marítim** and its invaluable collection of documents, maps and Navigation Laws. Farther along the water's edge, the wharves, the piers, the yachts riding anchor in the wet docks all continue the centuries-old maritime tradition of a city that once ruled the waters of the Mediterranean Sea, and sometimes, even those of the Oceans.

Top left, previous page, and this page, above and bottom: spectacular views of the beautiful, fascinating Plaça de Catalunya, which represents the beginning of the Ramblas.

Above centre: Joan Miró's famous, brightly coloured mosaic that enlivens the paving of the Plaça de la Boquería. Previous page, left: the Art Déco dragon that used to indicate an umbrella shop in the XVIII century Casa Bruno Quadros, between two of the street artists who are sometimes painted all over and resemble living statues; and bottom left, the striking monument to Columbus, which depicts the great navigator pointing towards the American continent.

The Triumphal Arch, designed by Josep Vilaseca i Casanovas and built in 1888 for the Universal Exhibition.

The monumental fountain in the park (below, a detail), made in 1888 by Josep Fontseré who was assisted by the still young and unknown Antoni Gaudí. The great Triumphal Arch is topped by Aurora and the Four-Horse Carriage, a statuary group forged in iron by Rossend Nobas. A fine statue of Venus stands over the water of the fountain.

Yet another part of Barcelona's Old City is equally fascinating and is ideal for those who love nature and are looking for a peaceful place to rest awhile among the greenery of a splendid park, one that can offer even moments of culture. This spot is reached through the *Plaça de l'Arc de Triomf*, with its monumental **gate** that was used as the entrance to the highly successful Universal Exhibition, held in Barcelona in 1888. The Arch was designed by Josep Vilaseca i Casanovas, and the friezes that ornate the upper part were made by Josep Reynés and Josep Llimona. This leads to the **Parc de la Ciutadela**, the site specially designed for the Universal Exhibition. Where elegant sculptures, a lake,

fountains, waterfalls and small woods can now be seen and where specimens of local flora flourish beside exotic species, a star-shaped military fortress once stood for centuries before being completely dismantled between 1869 and 1888 for this event. This Citadel, built between 1715 and 1720 and used as a prison for many years, was actually a series of buildings, including the *Arsenal* that has survived and which was adapted in 1932 to house the Catalan Parliament. There are many attractions in the park and beside the picturesque *fountain*, designed by Josep Fontseré with the help of the young Antoni Gaudí, the ones that stand out are the **Museu d'Art Modern de Catalunya**, one of the principal museums in the city holding work by XVIII-XX century Catalan artists (or those somehow connected with the region); the **Museu de Geología**, the oldest museum in Barcelona since it was opened in 1882, the same year that the park created in place of the old Citadel (which had been donate to the city) was opened to the public; the **Museu de Zoología**, housed in the picturesque *Castell dels Tres Dragons*, a building originally erected as a café-restaurant for the Universal Exhibition; and, naturally, the **Zoo** with its great number of animals, including a rare albino gorilla, the famous and much-loved *Floquet de Neu* (Snowflake).

Above, the MACBA and, bottom, the Palau del Mar, which holds the Museu d'Història de Catalunya. Left: a view of the Maremagnum, with the Aquarium.

However, over the past decades Barcelona has shown every intention of reserving more and more space for culture and the arts: an example of this is the **MACBA, Museu d'Art Contemporani de Barcelona**, housed in a sparkling white building that is, on its own, an example of modern art. It was opened in 1995 in Plaça dels Angels and exhibits collections of paintings and futuristic items by artists from Catalonia and from elsewhere; the works of art are continually updated and temporary exhibitions are held periodically.

While the 1888 Universal Exhibition left indelible signs in the fabric of Barcelona, the 1995 Olympic Games were undoubtedly an enormous contribution to the city's appearance on the threshold of the Third Millennium. One of the areas involved in the 'Olympic miracle' was the antique docklands, South of the Ramblas, an area full of significance in a city that had dominated the seas for centuries and in whose shipyards famous galleys were produced. Hence, many of the ancient buildings were renovat-ed and adapted for different usage, and new constructions were erected, so that **Port Vell** now appears very modern and futuristic. It starts at the **Moll d'Espanya** with its elegant structures; overlooking the wharf is the **Maremagnum**, a shopping mall and cultural centre containing an *Aquarium*, one of the largest in the world, a *library* specialised in general science and, in particular, marine subjects, a *video library*, numerous conference halls, one of the most up-to-date IMAX cinemas equipped with high standard technologies, bars, restaurants, meeting places and shops. The old fishermen's village is now the picturesque **Barceloneta**, a pleasant, lively district where cafés, restaurants, and fishing vessels riding anchor, all create the original atmosphere. Farther down the wharf stands the *Palau del Mar* that houses the **Museu d'Història de Catalunya**, a museum illustrating the history of this region from its origins to the present day by means of interactive techniques.

19

Casa Terrades, also known as Casa de les Punxes, designed by the architect Puig i Cadafalch.

The very original Hospital de la Santa Creu i de Sant Pau, by Lluís Domènech i Montaner.

A detail of the elegant Fundació Tàpies.

Though versatile and creative *par excellence*, Barcelona is distinct because of another peculiarity: the unusually high concentration of buildings and monuments in *Art Nouveau* style. In effect, this is the homeland of Modernism, which officially dates back to the decision made in 1854 to dismantle Barcelona's mediaeval walls in order to make space for urban expansion towards the centre and to occupy what had been for centuries an inaccessible military zone. This produced the **Eixample**, the modernistic district of Barcelona, originally designed by Ildefons Cerdà i Sunyer, a civil engineer

who was also responsible for the geometrical layout of the streets that cross each other perpendicularly, but which was further embellished between the end of the XIX century and the beginning of the XX century by many enthusiastic architects, the most important of whom was Lluís Domènech i Montaner, who also designed the **Hospital de la Santa Creu i de Sant Pau**. This new city hospital was started in 1902 and, in compliance with the architect's convictions that bright colours and great quantities of plants would have exerted a beneficial influence on the psychological wellbeing of the patients, and consequently on their health in general, the numerous buildings, walls and roofs were all painted in vivid hues, with *murals*, ceramic decorations, and surrounded by gardens. This same architect created another famous masterpiece, the **Palau de la Música Catalana** in the *Ciutat Vella*, not far from the *Eixample*. Therefore, the whole district, and especially the area better known as the *Quadrat d'Or*, is full of spectacular, delightful buildings: from the

famous **Fundació Tàpies** (1879) containing works of art by the famed surrealist artist, and from the **Casa Lleó Morera** (1902-1906), another of Lluís Domènech i Montaner's creations, to the Gothic-style **Casa Terrades**, better known as the *Casa de les Punxes* because of the many spires that crown it (1905), made of red brick and stone, and to the **Palau Baró** (1904) that houses the **Museu de la Música**, designed by yet another creative architect, Josep Puig i Cadafalch, to mention just a few. However, the entire *Eixample* is a flourish of elaborate decorations, brightly coloured tile facings and paving, skilfully worked stained-glass, spires and terraces, pinnacles and statues. And every corner seems to transmit the enthusiasm and ardour felt by all these artists when they created this very original part of Barcelona, artists who were morally supported and even financially sponsored by many upper class citizens, all enthralled by the new style and aspiring at having one of the Modernism works of art as their home.

The Sagrada Família

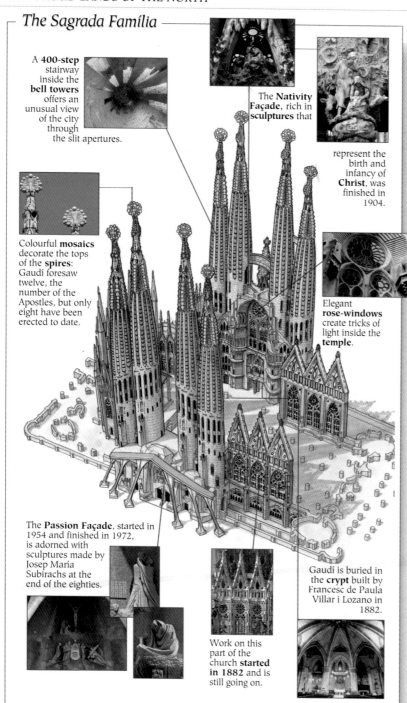

A **400-step** stairway inside the **bell towers** offers an unusual view of the city through the slit apertures.

The **Nativity Façade**, rich in **sculptures** that represent the birth and infancy of **Christ**, was finished in 1904.

A view of the Sagrada Família on the Nativity Façade side.

Pages 24-25: two details of the fine sculptures decorating the façades and spires.

Colourful **mosaics** decorate the tops of the **spires**: Gaudí foresaw twelve, the number of the Apostles, but only eight have been erected to date.

Elegant **rose-windows** create tricks of light inside the **temple**.

The **Passion Façade**, started in 1954 and finished in 1972, is adorned with sculptures made by Josep María Subirachs at the end of the eighties.

Work on this part of the church **started in 1882** and is still going on.

Gaudí is buried in the **crypt** built by Francesc de Paula Villar i Lozano in 1882.

Gaudí actually gave Barcelona his best masterpiece, the work of art he was to dedicate his working life to: the fantastic **Temple Expiatori de la Sagrada Família**. As a matter of fact, this building (financed by private money) had been already started in 1882, under the supervision of Francesc de Paula Villar i Lozano who had abandoned the task, however, due to increasing friction with the Barcelona Municipality. Approval of Gaudí's New-Gothic, floreate design was granted in 1883; from then on, this church was the centre and soul of this enthusiastic artist's life, becoming almost an obsession: he ended up investing all his own money in it, he lived inside it night and day, he went from house to house searching for donations and sponsorships to

Antoni Gaudí

Antoni Gaudí i Cornet was born in 1852 in Reus (Tarragona), but developed professionally and artistically in Barcelona (where he graduated in Architecture in 1878). Fascinated by New-Gothic and Moorish styles as well as being fond of lavish, brightly coloured decorations, he remains famous to this day for his skill in combining simple, basic materials (stone, wood, bricks) with fine wrought-iron, stained-glass, even ceramics, either in the form of tiles or tiny pieces linked together to form mosaics.

However, it would be impossible to talk about Modernism in Barcelona without mentioning the man who was undoubtedly the leader and chief representative of the movement, the imaginative and innovative artist who changed the appearance of the city. This is Antoni Gaudí i Cornet, born in 1852 in Reus (Tarragona) and trained in Barcelona, where he immediately found the ideal atmosphere and surroundings for him to manifest his unmistakable and overwhelming artistic talent.

Views of Gaudí's Barcelona. Clockwise from left to right: the Casa Batlló, the Casa Milà, showing details of the unusual chimneys on the latter and the arched, decorated rooftop of the former; the Parc Güell, with its distinct, brightly coloured signposts, and the famous sinusoidal bench, the biggest in the world.

help him finish the work, and when he was knocked down and killed by a tram in 1926, some believed that it was his obsession that had distracted him. Gaudí lived long enough to see only the apsis and one of the façades completed, besides the crypt, where he was eventually buried. Today, the Sagrada Família is still incomplete: nevertheless, in spite of construction being suspended during the Civil War, building has continued among much controversy but thanks to donations, and is still faithful to the design proposed by the great architect: there are now eight of the twelve elegant, very tall *spires* foreseen, the *Nativity Façade* in the East, the *Passion Façade* to the West, while work on the *Glory Façade* on the South side has still to begin, along with the central nave. The difficulties encountered during the construction of this masterpiece are illustrated in the very interesting **Museu de la Sagrada Família** in the crypt, and is full of Gaudí's drawings and plans. Prior to the church, however, the artist had already produced other famous buildings in the city: like the **Casa Milà**, also known as *La Pedrera*, built between 1906 and 1910 – heavily criticised at the time, decorated with wrought-iron balconies and astonish-

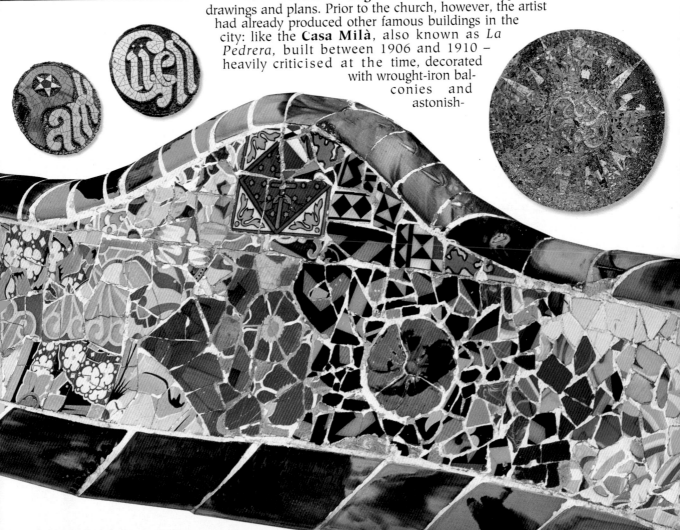

One of the sculptures in the Parc de l'Espanya Industrial.

ing chimneys, but also boasting a façade built with the curved outlines so dear to the artist –; the **Casa Batlló**, where the shiny, curved rooftops are fine examples of Gaudí's eccentric decorative style; the **Palau Güell**, built for the rich Count Eusebi Güell – a unique building where New-Gothic and Moorish styles blend and where wooden ceilings look down on wrought-iron lamps and ceramic decorations –; the **Parc Güell**, another feature made in 1890 for Count Güell, whose wish was to create a garden-city with many buildings immersed inside an Italian-style park: very little of this project was actually accomplished, though what was actually carried out was sufficient to make Parc Güell one of Gaudí's most imaginative and colourful creations, and it was here, among ceramic animals, glass mosaics and the longest *bench* in the world (sinusoidal in shape),

The sculpture by Roy Lichtenstein in Plaça d'Antoni López.

Modern and contemporary art in Barcelona: the Cat *by Botero.*

stood and now graced with streams, lakes and the works of art of many contemporary artists.

On the other hand, there are many areas in Barcelona that are fascinating and extremely interesting, even outside the Old City and nearer the outskirts. The large park on the **Montjuïc hill**, for example, is very attractive. On this hill that dominates the commercial port, where there was once a Celtiberian settlement and where, at a later date, the Romans built a temple for worshipping Jupiter (hence *Mons Jovis*, the original name of the hill), a castle was built in the XVII century and represented the first step of urbanisation of an area that had been neglected until then because of the total lack of water. However, both the Universal Exhibition in 1929 and the Olympic Games in 1992 brought decisive changes to the architecture of Montjuïc: today it boasts the **Fundació Joan Miró**, the **Museu Arqueològic**, the **Museu Nacional d'Art de Catalunya**, and the **Plaça d'Espanya** with its spectacular fountains, and even the characteristic **Poble Espanyol**, a park where typical buildings of the different Spanish regions have been reconstructed to produce a synthesis of the architectural styles throughout the country.

Another hill, or rather, a mountain range, farther away from the historical centre of Barcelona (but not less famous, however) deserves a visit: this is the **Tibidabo**, the peak of which can be reached by first taking the typical blue tram then, for the last part, the funicular railway. The name of the mountain comes from the Latin *tibi tabo*, the words which Satan used to tempt Christ when he took Him to a mountain top and promised Him the dominion of the world as far as the eye could see. The top of the Tibidabo is now dominated by the **Temple Expiatori del Sagrat Cor**, the Basilica of the Sacred Heart erected between 1902 and 1911 by Enric Sagnier. A *gigan-*

that the artist had his official residence for 20 years.

It may be said, though, that the whole of Barcelona has been able to reap the versatility and imagination generated by Modernism and make it its very own, winning the title of the liveliest city in Europe, as well as becoming an open-air museum of modern art. In fact, there are many squares, streets, gardens – the result of the city's policy to create more and more open spaces – where imposing, modernistic monuments are to be found, like the **Parc de Joan Miró**, also known as the *Parc de l'Escorxador* because this was once the site of the Barcelona slaughter-house, to name just one of the many. Created during the eighties, it is famous for Miró's huge statue called *Dona i Ocell* (1983), which stands 22 metres high in the middle of a pool and is covered in brightly coloured glazed tiles. Then there is the **Parc de l'Espanya Industrial**, another modern park created in the eighties where industries had previously

Parc de l'Escorxador: Dona i Ocell, *by Joan Miró, made with tiles modelled by Llorens-Artigas.*

tic statue of Christ is poised on the top of the central spire and a lift takes visitors up to the feet of the statue. However, the Tibidabo is also famous for the popular, forever crowded **Parc d'Atraccions**, the biggest fairground in Barcelona, opened in 1908. On another hill at the side of the mountain stands one of the most recent acquisitions of the city, the futuristic 288 metre high **Torre de Collserola**, another of the constructions made for the Olympic Games and now a modern observatory. There is a splendid panorama of the whole of Barcelona from its platform, spanning from the blue sea right round to the inland hills behind it.

The Temple Expiatori del Sagrat Cor, dominated by the spectacular statue of Christ, on the top of the Tibidabo.

A breathtaking view of Barcelona.

FIGUERES

Figueres is a pleasant town which nestles in the green, fertile inland of the Costa Brava, in the heart of its natural beauty; the town itself is famous for the great quantities of fruit and vegetables grown in its surrounding countryside, but it is even more renowned as the birthplace of Salvador Dalí.
In fact, besides the XVIII century **Castell de Sant Ferran** and the unique **Toy Museum** (*Museu de Joguets*), on the main street, Figueres is particularly esteemed for the much-visited **Dalí Theatre-Museum** (*Teatre-Museu Dalí*), planned personally by the artist in 1974 inside the old theatre of the

town. Here visitors can admire a highly significant selection of his work, while the building itself, with its very unusual features (an example is the huge hall where the overall effect of the decor makes it look like an enormous face), has become a splendid monument in its own right and a tribute to Dalí's unmistakable and original style.

The original exterior (above) and part of the interior (below) of the Dalí Theatre-Museum designed by the artist in 1974 and now one of the greatest sources of pride in Figueres. On the right, a detail from a poster illustrating an exhibition temporarily held in the museum, showing a portrait of the famous artist.

Salvador Dalí

Salvador Dalí, the incredibly prolific and audacious artist who ceaselessly searched for something different, who was forever driven by inborn forces to surprise and arouse the world (for which he was continuously the subject of debate and controversy), was born in Figueres in 1904; he was very attached to his home town even though he liked to stay in the nearby, splendid Cadaqués as well. This versatile artist, who never spurned experience in other fields as well, such as cinema and literature, after studying at the Madrid Academy of Art immediately attuned his spiritual and artistic lifestyle towards every possible type of experience, from Cubism to Futurism, from Metaphysics to Surrealism, which he revised in an extremely personal manner. It was this very complex personality that secured him success right from the start (his first exhibition was in 1919) and which continued to increase despite all the controversies, to the extent that by the time Dalí died in 1989 in Figueres, he had been already acclaimed one of the greatest and most interesting artists of the XX century.

COSTA BRAVA

Attractive inlets, green pine-woods, vineyards and olive groves bedecking the countryside, tiny harbours, beaches of powdery sand, and crystal clear sea: these are the distinguishing features of the almost 200 kilometres long Costa Brava, or the 'wild coast' as its name implies, an authentic paradise for tourists which was first launched in the sixties and has maintained its considerable popularity. In fact, what was once just a place for fishermen is now famous for some of the most popular and best equipped holiday resorts in the whole of Spain: **Blanes**, **Lloret de Mar**, **Tossa de Mar**, **Sant Feliu de Guixols**, **Platja d'Aro**, **Palamós**, **L'Escala**, **Roses** are only a few examples of the excellent tourist resorts where, next to golden sands and modern hotels, it is still possible to see the enchanting display of fishing nets drying in the breeze. There is also a series of charming and deserted little coves that should not be missed, like **Cala Pola** and **Cala Giverola**, so uncontaminated that they look really wild; but there are also pleasant, sun-drenched stretches of sand, at **Canyelles** and **Morsica** for example, that are undeniably attractive. Farther inland, tiny mediaeval villages like **Pals** and **Peratallada**, their austere grace intact, cling to the rugged slopes which dominate the coastline and inlets. And then, thirty kilometres from the sea sits ancient **Gerona**, head city of the province and dating back to pre-Roman times, since its birth accustomed to the typical life of a city on the borders, a fortified stronghold defending the entire peninsula, capable of defying umpteen sieges (one of which was the lengthy attack by Philip III the Bold, King of France), protected behind sturdy, imposing walls. The ancient splendour of the city can still be seen in its exquisite *Cathedral*, erected over a primitive Romanesque temple and one of the finest examples of Catalan Gothic, but nevertheless embellished with touches of more recent Baroque magnificence. The octagonal *Bell-tower* that rises on the right-hand side is known as the 'Charlemagne Tower' and was added on during the XVI century. Other, numerous examples of Romanesque architecture worth seeing are the churches dedicated to **San Nicolás** and **San Pedro de Galligans**, or the **Baños Arabes** which were originally reserved for the rich Moorish craftsmen and businessmen who still prospered in Gerona almost five centuries after the *Reconquista*, and the old Jewish quarters, **El Call**, a typical example of Mediterranean mediaeval architecture.

Modern facilities, crowded beaches and small tourist ports make a striking background to the more traditional scenes of fishing nets laid out to dry.

that recall both cultures, in spite of the devastation inflicted on it during the War of Independence in the XIX century. For example, the elegant XI century palace, the **Alfajería**, which was chosen by the Catholic Monarchs as their residence and later became the headquarters of the Inquisition, was erected by the Moors. While the two majestic **Cathedrals** that tower over two sides of the main square in Zaragoza were built by Christians. The first of these, **La Seo**, is a blend of styles and was built in the XII century over an already existing mosque. The other one, the **Basílica de Nuestra Señora del Pilar** with its 11 *domes*, is dedicated to the patron saint of Spain and holds the *Santa Capilla*. Here worshipers venerate a small *wooden statue* of the Virgin Mary that stands high on top of an alabaster column, and which is dressed in precious robes that are changed every day. The climax of his particular devotion to the Madonna del Pilar is on 12th October, when the *Fiesta del Pilar* is celebrated with much pomp and merriment by the entire city.

The battle of Zaragoza

On the 20th August 1701, the imperial troops of Archduke Charles, pretender to the throne, triumphed over Philip of Bourbon and his men in an important victory for Zaragoza. Accounts of this battle, which was one of the empire's last successes in Spain, spread far and wide and it was commemorated even with works of art, such as this 171 x 257 cm oil painting by Jean Pierre Bredael, now in the Heeresgeschichtliches Museum in Vienna.

ZARAGOZA

The remains of the forum and part of the walls are all that is left of Roman *Caesaraugusta*, which was founded over an even older settlement during the first century BC on the banks of the river Ebro. However, this was the original nucleus that was to become modern Zaragoza. After suffering occupation by the Moors in the VIII century and then reclaimed by the Christian army of Alphonse I in the XII century, the expanding city savoured the peaceful and profitable cohabitation of the two religious groups for centuries thereafter. Hence, this austere capital of Aragona is still famed for splendid monuments

The majestic outline of the Basilica de Nuestra Señora del Pilar, dedicated to the Virgin, patron of Spain, dominates Zaragoza from all four sides with its eleven domes and its unmistakable brightly coloured roof-tiles. Devoted pilgrims constantly visit the church to worship the famous wooden statue of the Virgin Mary.

Francisco Goya

A contribution to the lustre of Zaragoza was undoubtedly that brought by one of its most distinguished citizens, Francisco Goya, who was born in Fuendetodos in 1746 and became famous as the official painter of the Spanish Court (his portraits of King Charles IV and his family are very well-known). Goya started his career by designing the basic cartoons (preparatory drawings) for tapestries, and then he took part in decorating the Basílica de Nuestra Señora del Pilar in Zaragoza. He distinguished himself particularly because of the considerable amount of work he produced which, as time went by, was more and more influenced both by his private life (he became melancholic and an introvert due to his progressive deafness) and by the devastating events of that period: the invasion of Napoleon's troops in Spain, and all the horrors they disseminated, seems to have impelled him to depict subjects burdened with suffering and menaced by the dark shadows of foreboding tragedy. Goya subsequently settled in France and died in Bordeaux in 1828.

OLITE

While Navarra is one of the acclaimed historical centres in Spain, the small but attractive town of Olite, immersed in the vivid greenery of its vineyards, has been its pulsating heart for centuries. In fact, it was here in this town, originally a Roman settlement but which developed greatly during mediaeval times, that the sovereigns of Navarra decided to establish their residence in the XV century. This decision gave rise to the august **Palacio Real de Olite**, a real fortified castle, which Charles III the Nobleman started in 1406; the ramparts, towers, turrets and crenellated sentry-walks along the battlements of the menacing façade are counterbalanced by the exquisitely spacious and elegant interiors, richly decorated with ceramics and elaborate carvings. After being ransacked many times and having undergone restoration during the first half of the XX century, the manor stills majestically dominates the labyrinth of ancient narrow streets, steps and little squares which distinguishes the dense structure of Olite. Part of the town is still closed within the old walls and preserves other ancient treasures which deserve a visit, like the III century **Convent of the Clarisse Nuns** and, above all, the **Iglesia de Santa María la Real**, an ancient royal chapel built in the XIV century and very much admired for its extraordinary and exquisitely created Gothic *doorway*.

Imposing towers and turrets enhance the sturdy Palacio Real de Olite, completely reconstructed during the XX century.

Santa María la Real, the XIV century chapel famous for its beautiful Gothic doorway capped by an elaborately sculptured lunette.

PAMPLONA

Pamplona is a hard-working city and although it has been significantly industrialised over the past decades, it nevertheless remains jealously attached to its ancient historical roots. Known in Roman times as 'Pompeo's City', called after its probable founder, the fortress city of Pamplona lived its greatest moments of splendour between the X and XVI centuries, when it was the capital of the Kingdom of Navarra. The focal point of the city is the **Plaza del Castillo**, with the princely **Palacio de Navarra** and its opulent *Throne Room*; the **Paseo de Sarasate** leads off from the square and reaches the church of **San Nicolás** (XIII century) and the star-shaped fortified **Ciudadela** (Citadel) built for King Philip II during the VI century. The majestic IV century **Cathedral** stands not far from the ancient walls (*Murallas*) and, while originally built along Gothic lines, it now features a XVIII century *façade* by the neo-classic architect, Ventura Rodríguez. Inside there are the two splendid alabaster *tombs* of Charles III the Noble, King of Navarra, and of his wife, Eleonora. Another very interesting feature, beyond the mediaeval *Puerta de la Preciosa*, is the attractive Gothic *cloister* with its elegant fretwork decorations.

One of the other buildings worthwhile visiting is the picturesque **Ayuntamiento**, the Baroque Municipal Hall; a rocket is traditionally launched from its balcony every year, to announce the beginning of the *Fiesta de Los Sanfermines*. Definitely worth seeing, is the rich **Museo de Navarra**, where one can roam through the archaeology, history and art of Navarra and of the whole of Spain. Besides the *archaeological relics* kept in the VI century hospital which houses the museum, there are splendid *Roman mosaics* of Islamic inspiration, *frescoes* removed from local Romanesque churches, an admirable collection of *paintings by Basque artists* and Goya's famous *portrait of Marquis de San Adrián*.

The solemn façade of Pamplona Cathedral.

Hemingway's Spain

Ernest Hemingway (1898-1961), the great American novelist and journalist, was linked to the very soul of Spain and its people by a web of fine threads woven over the years. Hemingway, who had an unquenchable thirst for adventure and discovery, participated in the Spanish Great Civil War as a correspondent and did not hesitate to join the antifrancoist ranks.

This experience affected him greatly; however, the intriguing fascination of Spain had already won the heart of this man who had already lived in the Iberian country. Though Hemingway dedicated one of his masterpieces, *For whom the bell tolls* (1940), to the Civil War, it was another aspect of Spanish life that completely seduced him: bullfighting, and bulls. He looked upon this confrontation between man and bull, as the struggle man has to face day after day in the bullring of life. And on account of this, he dedicated his famous essay-novel *Death in the afternoon* (1932) to the bullfight, its heroes and its traditions.

The extraordinary atmosphere sensed in the streets of Pamplona during the exciting bull race had already been highlighted in *The sun also rises* (1926), which, incidentally, is also known as *Fiesta*.

THE BULL RACE

'The fiesta had really begun. It went on, day and night, for seven days. The dancing went on, drinking went on, and the noise never stopped for a week. The things that happened could only happen during a fiesta. Everything became unreal and it seemed that nothing could have any consequence. [...] It was a fiesta, and it continued for seven days'.
Ernest Hemingway,
The sun also rises.

When talking about Spain and bulls, the subject is not always the bullfight. In fact, folklore and tradition intertwine every year in the streets of Pamplona for one of the most spectacular events, one that is longed for not only by the inhabitants: this is the traditional *Encierro*, the fantastic, exciting bull race. The *Encierro* is the climax of

the *Fiesta de Los Sanfermines* (called after San Fermín, the Patron Saint) whom the town celebrates from 6th - 14th July. For just over a week, therefore, the normally tranquil and industrial capital of Navarra is literally in turmoil: eight days of singing, dancing, merriment and, above all, of challenging bulls. While the excited crowd becomes enraptured and delirious, six bulls are freed into the streets of the old part of the city, where they chase the courageous *Sanfermines*, who naturally pray to their Patron Saint for protection in this particularly difficult moment. In effect, the Pamplona *Fiesta* has fundamentally religious origins, so it also foresees throngs of worshipers flanking the solemn procession that takes the statue of San Firmino on a 'pilgrimage' from one church to another. But, at the end of this astonishing week, the tough nature of the local people melts and relaxes in the intense emotion of the last night of the *Fiesta*, when everybody goes down to the main square to sing folksongs in the warm, flickering light of candles.

RONCESVALLES

The tiny town called Roncesvalles, known in history for the heroic battle campaigned there in 778 by Charlemagne's soldiers, who were attacked and decimated by infidels, owed its fortune to being a compulsory stop for French pilgrims on their way over the Pyrenees to Santiago de Compostela.

The two most important monuments in Roncesvalles are, in fact, typically religious ones: the **Augustine Monastery**, and the XIII century **Colegiata Real**, a Gothic church that for centuries offered hospitable shelter to the pilgrims, who could worship the beautiful, silver *Virgin Mary and Child* there. Moreover, King Sancho VII the Powerful is buried in an imposing *tomb* in the *Chapter Room*.

Daylight filters in colourful rays through a splendid *stained-glass window* depicting the Battle of Las Navas de Tolosa (1212), in which Christian armies (including those of the King of Navarra) finally triumphed over the Almohadi Arabian military forces.

The austere religious architecture typical of Roncesvalles.

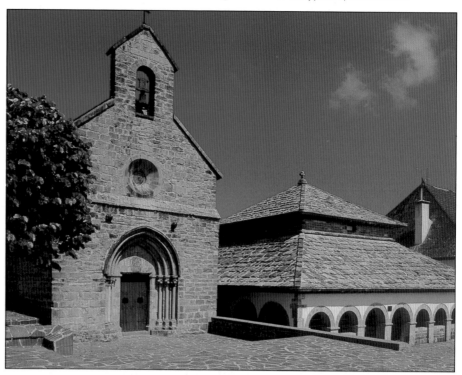

The rack and ruin of Roncesvalles

The *Chanson de Roland* (XII century) narrates of how valiant Orlando, the invincible hero of the poem of chivalry, met his death in 778 during the famous battle in Roncesvalles. After being betrayed by Gano (the ambassador sent by Charlemagne to Marsilio, the conquered pagan King of Zaragoza to whom the conditions for peace had already been dictated), Orlando, who had been assigned the rear lines of the homeward-bound Frank army, was ambushed by Marsilio's troops right in Roncesvalles. In spite of every effort to ward them off, the hero died together with all his men. Charlemagne himself could do nothing to help them, since the sound of Orlando's horn reached him too late: all he could do was weep over his dead paladin and swear merciless vengeance for him.

The death of Orlando, XIV century, *Castres, Municipal Library.*

Puente la Reina

There are many places in Navarra that owe their fame to ancient traditions or historical events. One of these is certainly Puente la Reina, on the road to Santiago de Compostela. In this case, the actual name of the town describes its setting, with its imposing arched **footbridge** built by royal order in the XI century to facilitate pilgrims crossing the river Arga. Nearby stands the **Iglesia de Santiago**, which conserves a unique statue of the Saint depicted as a pilgrim.

The ancient and audacious construction over the River Arga that gave Puente la Reina its name.

The awesome and austere Castillo de Javier where St. Francesco Saverio was born.

Javier

There is a castle in Navarra, the XIII century **Castillo de Javier**, in which a man who was destined to leave an indelible mark in the history of Christianity was born during the first years of the XVI century: Francesco Saverio, now Patron Saint of Navarra, who founded the Society of Jesus together with St. Ignatius Loyola. The large castle is practically now a mausoleum to his memory and a community of Jesuits actually inhabit it; visitors can see the Saint's bedroom, a museum dedicated to this personality, and also a beautiful oratory with a polychromatic *crucifix* made in the XIII century.

BILBAO

Proud or susceptible, just as its almost 400,000 inhabitants are, Bilbao is a typical, northern Basque city that has been capable of gleaning a solid and enviable well-being from its large fishing-port, iron mines, chemical industries and steel-works, especially from the XIX century onwards (when Basque bankers, ship-owners and merchants represented financial power in Spain). Behind the grey, drear barrier of industrial plants, however, the IV century **Old City** (*Casco Viejo*) sits on the west bank of the Rio Nervíon; this ancient fishing village, with its network of narrow streets huddled around the *Basílica de Santiago*, only partly escaped destruction during the various wars.

Famous for its museums (**Museo Arqueológico Etnográfico e Histórico Vasco**, and **Museo de Bellas Artes**, which boasts some of the richest collections in the whole of Spain), Bilbao is now at the centre of an ambitious plan for reorganisation and development which, after adroitly overcoming the worrying problem of environmental pollution and after presenting the city with a new subway line, has now given the city another jewel: the futuristic **Guggenheim Museum**. This was opened in 1997 for exhibiting modern and contemporary art, though it is already considered a masterpiece in its own right because of the remarkable, unusual building which houses it: designed by the American architect, Frank Gehry, who freely interpreted the shape of a ship, the museum is outstanding because of its shiny, unmistakable *façade* covered in titanium, its spectacular *entrance hall* which soars 60 metres high, the *terraces*, the *water-garden,* and the whole construction – a unique monument to modern architecture which can be seen from all four corners of the city.

The futuristic titanium exterior of the Museum.

BASQUE FISHERMEN

Practically all of the Basque coastline is dotted here and there with typical fishermen's villages and one of the main resources of the entire region, in fact, has always been its fishing industry; but it must not be forgotten that the Basques have distinguished themselves since ancient times as expert and daring seamen as well. Their proud, hardy character braced them as they sailed and defied the seas. Indeed, many of the sailors who boarded the ships sailing towards the New World during the years immediately after Columbus had discovered it, were actually Basques. And when it comes to fishing, the Basque skill cannot be denied. Accordingly, though the nearby Bay of Biscay has always been rich in excellent fish, they have braved the icy, stormy deep waters of the Atlantic Ocean to catch cod and whales since man can remember. On their return to land, they then enjoy a supper of fresh fish accompanied by a satisfying plate of vegetables.

GUERNICA

A tragic event in Basque modern history is the subject of one of Pablo Picasso's masterpieces, a 351 x 782 cm oil painting kept for a long time in the Museum of Modern Art in New York and now prime exhibit in the Centro de Arte Reina Sofía in Madrid: *Guernica*.

On 26th April 1937, during the Civil War, the Basque town called Guernica y Luno was completely destroyed by German bombers. One month after the tragedy, the artist commemorated the sacrifice by painting this work of art for the Spanish stand in the Paris Universal Exhibition. Letting his cubism experience fade into diffused surrealism, he was able to grasp and transmit the anguish of tragedy and destruction by depicting houses on fire, terrified horses and the symbolic presence of a Minotaur, the emblem of blind fury.

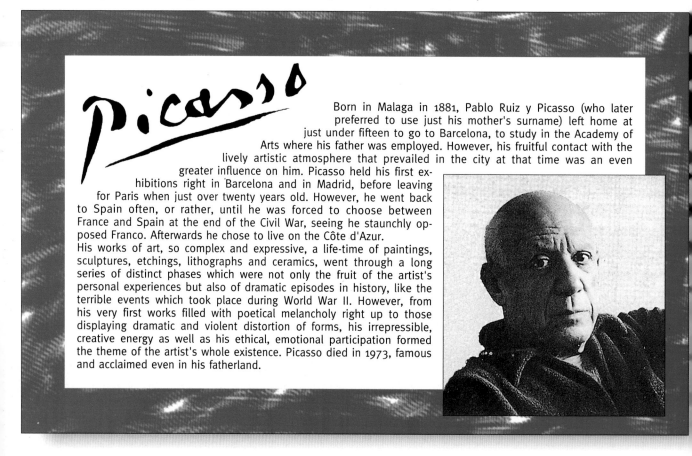

Born in Malaga in 1881, Pablo Ruiz y Picasso (who later preferred to use just his mother's surname) left home at just under fifteen to go to Barcelona, to study in the Academy of Arts where his father was employed. However, his fruitful contact with the lively artistic atmosphere that prevailed in the city at that time was an even greater influence on him. Picasso held his first exhibitions right in Barcelona and in Madrid, before leaving for Paris when just over twenty years old. However, he went back to Spain often, or rather, until he was forced to choose between France and Spain at the end of the Civil War, seeing he staunchly opposed Franco. Afterwards he chose to live on the Côte d'Azur.

His works of art, so complex and expressive, a life-time of paintings, sculptures, etchings, lithographs and ceramics, went through a long series of distinct phases which were not only the fruit of the artist's personal experiences but also of dramatic episodes in history, like the terrible events which took place during World War II. However, from his very first works filled with poetical melancholy right up to those displaying dramatic and violent distortion of forms, his irrepressible, creative energy as well as his ethical, emotional participation formed the theme of the artist's whole existence. Picasso died in 1973, famous and acclaimed even in his fatherland.

SAN SEBASTIÁN

One of the most famous, lively and animated cities in the whole of Spain is to be found in the Basque region: San Sebastián. Nestling in its splendid bay, protected by a circlet of mountains and hills topped by Monte Urgull, facing the graceful Isla de Santa Clara sitting out at sea, this is one of the cities preferred by tourists for its beaches and its modern facilities. The city's fortune began at the end of the XIX century, when Spanish aristocracy started choosing this beautiful place for holidays and amusement following Queen María Cristina's decision to build the famous **Palacio Miramar** here – which the royal family still inhabit and enjoy. Very little of the old city remains to this day, since a devastating fire destroyed many of the buildings in 1813. All the same, la **Parte Vieja**, the 'Old City', still maintains its personal allure with its narrow streets, the *fish market* and the characteristic taverns and cafés.

The historical heart of the city is right here, the **Plaza de la Constitución**, surrounded by porticoes surmounted by houses and enhanced by conspicuous windows with blue and orange shutters. For a long time, this square was the bullring and to this day numbers can still be seen on the balconies, because

these were 'reserved' and 'rented' for the occasion. Not far away is one of the very few XVIII century buildings still standing in the city, the superb **Basílica de Santa María del Coro**, with its elegant Baroque *doorway*.
However, the real protagonist in San Sebastián is unquestionably the sea that rolls its waves on to sun-drenched beaches, like the wide **Playa de la Concha**, the very popular **Playa de Ondarreta**,

and the delightful **Playa de la Zurriola**, all dazzling white and stretched out at the foot of the mountains, from Monte Igueldo to Monte Ulía; together with the beautiful, luxurious hotels they contribute to making San Sebastián one of the most fashionable resorts in the whole of Spain, as well as a place for mass tourism.
However, the sea also means fishing, boats, sea life: from the **old port** to the **Palacio del Mar** – built in

1828 by the architect Juan Carlos Guerra and now site of the **Aquarium**, an interesting museum dedicated to Basque naval history , there are many opportunities for knowing more about this aspect of life in San Sebastián.

Life here is animated more than ever now through a series of interesting initiatives and important international events: the **Jazz Festival** in July, the **Semana Grande** around mid-August celebrating Basque folklore and tradition, the **Classic Music Festival** at the end of August, and the famous **Film Festival,** one of the most important in Europe, held every year at the end of September since 1953. All occasions which liven up an already vivacious Summer atmosphere in this delightful Basque city.

Transparent sea, sun-kissed beaches, pretty little ports, pleasant inlets, splendid buildings facing directly onto the seafront: this is the secret of San Sebastián's fascination and the explanation of how it has seduced aristocratic (and not only) tourists for over a century.

THE PICOS DE EUROPA

Magnificent and imposing, often snow-capped even in Summer, the Picos de Europa mountains soar majestically to separate the Asturias and Cantabrian coastline from the inland Castile and León plateaux. Their name traditionally derives from the fact that their peaks are so high (some are even over 2,500 metres) that navigators far out at sea could see them and know that land was near at last. The beautiful rural scenery of bright green valleys, crystal-clear streams, deep gorges, groups of rustic stone-built dwellings, pasture-land grazed by small herds (the famous *cabrales* cheese, a creamy blue cheese made with cow, goat and sheep milk, is produced here), splendid lakes like *Lago de la Ercina* and *Lago Enol*, both of glacier origin, is an authentic natural heritage to be protected and conserved. The largest nature park in the whole of Europe, the Parque Nacional de Covadonga, was established for this reason; the park is named after the place where there is a famous *sanctuary* with an elegant neo-Romanesque *basilica* built between the end of the XIX century and the turn of the XX century, and where legends narrate that in 722 Pelayo, a Visigoth nobleman who was to become King of Asturias (a large statue commemorates him here), leading a handful of heroic warriors warded off the attack of a whole army of Moors.

SANTILLANA DEL MAR

Time seems to be at a standstill in Santillana, the picturesque mediaeval town in Cantabria: austere stone cottages, cobbled streets, coats-of-arms on the outside walls and sedate porticoes are all jealously conserved intact in the oldest part of the town (dedicated to and named after St. Juliana) that now attracts a great number of tourists drawn by the natural beauty of the nearby coast.

An ancient and famous monument stands out in the heart of mediaeval Santillana: the Romanesque **Colegiata**. This was built between the XII and XIII centuries to house the worshipped remains of Juliana the Martyr; the entrance is through an artistic *doorway* framed by a round arch, and once inside visitors can walk around the splendid *cloisters* and admire the famous *capitals* skilfully adorned with relief sculptures of biblical scenes. In the main square of the town, a XV century stone

Of all the many, notable features in the spectacular Colegiata de Santillana del Mar, particular mention must be made of the impressive cloisters and, above all, the capitals of the columns that surround it, skilfully sculptured with lively Biblical scenes.

The Altamira Caves

One of the jewels of Cantabria is definitely the **Cuevas de Altamira**, the famous caves where, in 1869, the little daughter of a local landowner discovered by chance some outstanding *rock paintings* and *engravings*, Palaeolithic polychromatic works of art dating back to 18,000 - 13,000 BC For a long time, their authenticity was debated because they were so beautifully painted, so detailed, so skilfully coloured with pigments: deer, horses, boars and, especially bisons, all seem to saunter along the rough walls. However, similar drawings, discovered at the beginning of the XX century in caves that had been previously inaccessible, demonstrated that those found in Altamira

One of the famous, brightly coloured bisons painted by incredibly talented artists on the walls of the Altamira Caves in prehistoric times.

were unquestionably painted by very talented 'prehistoric artists'. Visiting the caves is quite difficult at present: access is restricted in order to protect the integrity of the treasures inside and visits must be booked well in advance.

To compensate this, however, the cave masterpieces and their history are now illustrated in great detail in the **Museo de Altamira** in Santillana.

palace now houses a well-known **Parador** (state-owned hotel), named after Gil Blas who was the main character in the XVIII century tale *Gil Blas de Santillana*, written by Alain-René Lesage, and in a similar story in verse by Victor Hugo. Not far from the centre is the Convent de Regina Cœli, which is the site of an interesting **Diocesan Museum.**

The beautifully preserved Colegiata de Santillana del Mar still displays its austere Romanesque elegance, a significant contribution to which is the graceful entrance-door, framed within a series of blind round arches. Two stone lions still guard over the pilgrims coming to worship St. Juliana's tomb.

San Beato de Liébana

Lost in the wilds of the Picos de Europa in Cantabria, not far from the ancient city of Potes, there is a VII century monastery (rebuilt completely in the XIII century) that proudly guards a fragment of the Holy Cross: **Santo Toribio de Liébana**. This was the peaceful, sacred place where San Beato de Liébana lived in the VIII century; the monk became famous as the author of a *Commentary on the Apocalypse*, which was copied many times and splendidly illustrated.

Commentary on the Apocalypse
*by San Beato de Liébana,
X century, Madrid,
Escorial Library.*

Rows of vines growing in Rioja Alavesa (left), casks kept in underground cellars (above) and top quality wine: these are some of the most traditional features of the famous Rioja wine-growing district.

IN THE WINE REGION: LA RIOJA

Of the many, highly appreciated wine-growing districts that are a source of pride to Spain, one of the most famous is definitely Rioja, right next to the Basque Country and not far from the Pyrenees, where the tepid Mediterranean climate of the Ebro valley blends with the rainy Atlantic climate typical of the mountainous area reaching farther South, almost parallel to the course of the river itself. In its midst there are wide, fertile valleys, unmistakable because of the enormous stretches of vineyards with vines planted row after row towards the horizon, as far as the eye can see.

The whole region, which is divided into three separate and distinct wine-growing areas, **Rioja Alta**, **Rioja Baja** and **Rioja Alavesa**, produces particularly characteristic, first class wines: the red wines are very well known, generally suitable for ageing, often intensely aromatic and made from different types of grapes (though the *Tempranillo* is the variety of red grape most typical of the Rioja area), while the white wines are equally appreciated, as are the less common rosé wines which are made mainly of *Garnacha* grapes. All the different stages in production, from growing the vines right up to bottling, still strictly follow traditional methods such as ageing the wines in sturdy oak barrels kept in the typical, dark underground cellars where appropriate and constant levels of humidity and temperature are guaranteed: hence, traditions which have never changed over the centuries, yet another source of pride for what is rightly called 'The Home of Spanish Wine'.

Spectacular rocky shores with small, deserted beaches hiding amongst the greenery of the inlets are the most appreciated features of the Asturias coast, washed by an extraordinarily clear sea teeming with fish.

ASTURIAS: WHERE NATURE MEETS HISTORY

Lying between the Bay of Biscay abounding in fish and the impressive peaks of the Cordillera Cantábrica, the Asturias region is a strip of land stretching from East to West and nowadays a principality under the direct patronage of the heir to the throne of Spain whose title is, in fact, Prince of Asturias. For a long time, Asturias took advantage of the natural protection and isolation offered by the mountain ridges behind it and remained independent, capable of warding off even the Moors. And the Christian kingdom established here in the VIII century reached vertices of true splendour, which can be seen to this day in the many ancient churches scattered here and there, severe and impressive, and in the austere, imposing buildings in the elegant cities. Along the high, rugged coast, there are beaches and coves that have become sheltered har-

bours for fishing boats and popular tourist resorts. Inland, the countryside in the range of hills bordering the mountains has always been particularly suitable for agriculture and animal breeding. In the valleys wedged between the mountain peaks, the hardworking, determined inhabitants are still attached to antique traditions and a particular form of craftsmanship that have been handed down throughout the centuries. In some parts of the inland district they even speak an ancient dialect, spoken only in the Asturian countryside and called *bable*. The principal city of the region is Oviedo, which nestles amongst the bright green hills; the typical drink here is its famous *cider*, not just made here but also drunk in great quantities and on every possible occasion: it even has its rôle in the delicious *caldereta*, an Asturian fish soup made with cod, sea-urchins, various types of shell-fish and, of course, the ever-present cider.

Wooded mountains and snow-capped peaks feature in the other part of Asturias, the wild, rough inland, where the inhabitants jealously hang on to traditions and customs that have never changed over the centuries.

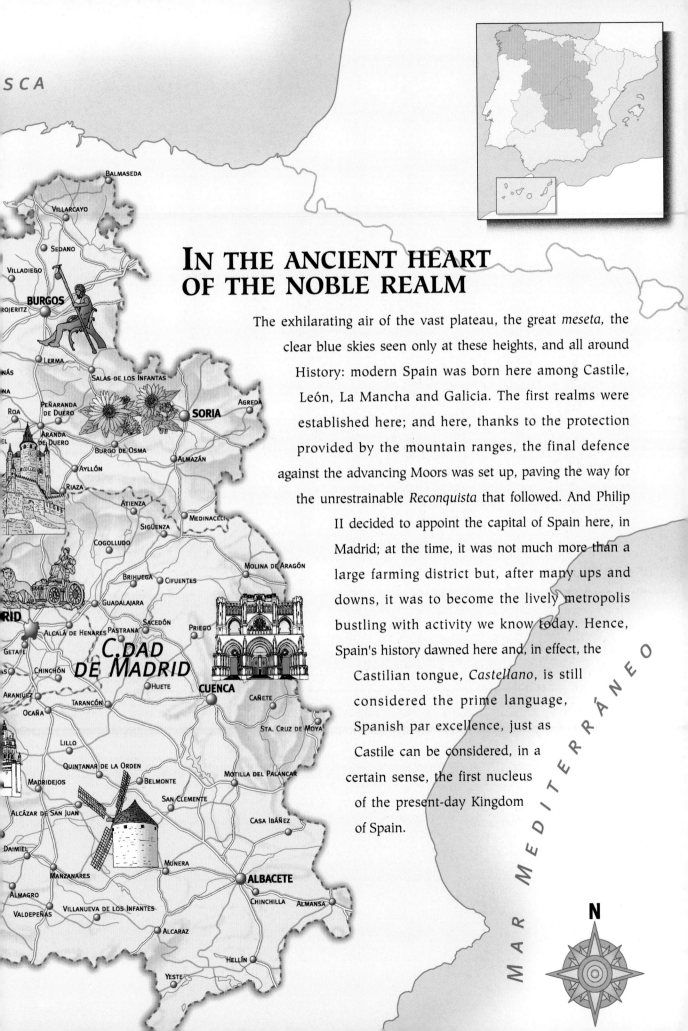

IN THE ANCIENT HEART OF THE NOBLE REALM

The exhilarating air of the vast plateau, the great *meseta*, the clear blue skies seen only at these heights, and all around History: modern Spain was born here among Castile, León, La Mancha and Galicia. The first realms were established here; and here, thanks to the protection provided by the mountain ranges, the final defence against the advancing Moors was set up, paving the way for the unrestrainable *Reconquista* that followed. And Philip II decided to appoint the capital of Spain here, in Madrid; at the time, it was not much more than a large farming district but, after many ups and downs, it was to become the lively metropolis bustling with activity we know today. Hence, Spain's history dawned here and, in effect, the Castilian tongue, *Castellano*, is still considered the prime language, Spanish par excellence, just as Castile can be considered, in a certain sense, the first nucleus of the present-day Kingdom of Spain.

SCA

BALMASEDA
VILLARCAYO
SEDANO
VILLADIEGO
BURGOS
ROJERITZ
LERMA
NÁS
SALAS DE LOS INFANTAS
AGREDA
ROA
PEÑARANDA DE DUERO
SORIA
NA
ARANDA DEL DUERO
BURGO DE OSMA
EL
ALMAZÁN
AYLLÓN
RIAZA
ATIENZA
MEDINACELI
SIGÜENZA
COGOLLUDO
MOLINA DE ARAGÓN
BRIHUEGA
CIFUENTES
GUADALAJARA
RID
SACEDÓN
PASTRANA
PRIEGO
ALCALÁ DE HENARES
C.DAD DE MADRID
GETAFE
AS
CHINCHÓN
HUETE
CUENCA
ARANJUEZ
TARANCÓN
CAÑETE
OCAÑA
STA. CRUZ DE MOYA
LILLO
QUINTANAR DE LA ORDEN
MADRIDEJOS
BELMONTE
MOTILLA DEL PALANCAR
SAN CLEMENTE
ALCÁZAR DE SAN JUAN
CASA IBÁÑEZ
DAIMIEL
MUNERA
MANZANARES
ALBACETE
ALMAGRO
VILLANUEVA DE LOS INFANTES
CHINCHILLA
ALMANSA
VALDEPEÑAS
ALCARAZ
HELLÍN
YESTE

MAR MEDITERRÁNEO

N

GALICIA, THE FISHING REGION

The clear, cold waters of the Atlantic Ocean which roll on to the rugged Galicia shores, deeply carved with inlets called *rías*, are incredibly abundant in fish. In fact, over half of Spain's fishing fleets anchor in Galicia and more than half of the fish caught in the whole of Spain ends up in Galician nets. Besides being plentiful, Galician fish is also extremely tasty: the local dishes bear witness to this and although they are simply cooked, their appetising flavour has earned them great success. Cod, hake, anglerfish, sole and octopus are bountiful at the family table and in Galician restaurants. But the real specialities of the area are clams, muscles and sea-food in general: the special, partly submerged platforms used for breeding these species can be seen all along the coast and in the beautiful inlets. These delicacies are then gathered by the local women, usually during the month of November, and are mainly for export. However, they are the real protagonists in Galician cookery, used in practically every recipe.

SANTIAGO DE COMPOSTELA

The ancient Route to Santiago, which extends for hundreds of miles, has been one of the main routes for pilgrimages in the western world since the beginning of mediaeval times to this day. The route meanders through wonderful scenery full of mediaeval castles, Romanesque and Gothic cathedrals, monasteries and cities that are still protected behind sturdy walls. Tradition relates that the body of the James the Elder, the Apostle who spent six years praying in Spain after Christ's crucifixion and who was subsequently martyred in Palestine in the year 44, was brought to Galicia in ancient times. And it miraculously came to light in the IX century (in 813, to be precise) when an ancient Roman tomb was discovered. This sepulchre and the increasing devotion shown towards the sacred remains made Santiago de Compostela flourish; the name includes that of the Apostle Saint and reference to the legend whereby the location of the tomb is supposed to have been indicated to the Galician Bishop, Teodomiro, by means of a brightly shining star (*campus stellae*). Hence, Santiago became first a symbol of Christian resistance, then the symbol of the glorious *Reconquista*. Devastated by the Normans, then by the Moors in 997 who set fire to the Cathedral, it was rebuilt at the beginning of the XI century, and from then on its growth and development never encountered obstacles again: in Mediaeval times, because of the widely spreading faith in St. James and the strong religious enthusiasm which accompanied the Spanish *Reconquista*, Santiago rapidly became the destination of the most famous and popular Christian pilgrimages after those to Rome and Jerusalem, with an average of half a million pilgrims visiting it every year. Precise itineraries led pilgrims to the sacred destination: the first of these was the so-called 'French Route or *Camino*' that started in Aquisgrana (Aachen) then went through Paris, Orléans, Bordeaux and Roncesvalles, and ran parallel to the less famous Aragonese route. While guide-books were continuously produced in various languages to inform pilgrims of the various canonical halts along the route (the first was written by a French monk called Aymeric Picaud, while Pope Callisto II officially approved the *Camino* as an initiatory

route towards the sacred city), numerous hospices and oratories dedicated to the Saint appeared along the way, trading flourished and the various cultures spread rapidly. And once the pilgrims reached Santiago, they walked through the historical centre, down the narrow streets and across the typical mediaeval squares until they came to the spectacular **Cathedral** with its Baroque façade, in the beautiful *Praza do Obradoiro*, the traditional meeting-point for all pilgrims. The structure of the sacred building, one of the largest in Christendom, is still that erected between the XI and XII centuries over the remains of the small temple ordered by Alphonse II to hold the Apostle's tomb, but the exterior was remodelled at various moments in history, resulting in the richly adorned western *façade* and the 74-metre high twin *towers* (XVIII century). A XII century addition was the famous *Pórtico de Gloria*, the historical entrance door for pilgrims, framed with statues of prophets and apostles, whereas an XI century refinement was the *Porta das Praterias*, decorated with interesting bas-relief sculptures depicting scenes from the *Bible*. Once inside, the pilgrims show their devotion by kissing the XIII century *statue of St. James* that stands behind the main altar, covered with a silver cloak, then they pay homage to the Saint's remains, which are supposed to lie in the *Crypt* underneath the altar, buried within the IX century foundations. Many of the historical buildings in Santiago are dedicated to the pilgrims and to the religious essence that pervades the area: from the **Convento de San Martín Pinario** with its elegant Baroque church, to the **Hostal de los Reyes Católicos**, built by the monarchs to offer pilgrims appropriate accommodation, from the **Convento de San Paio de Antealtares**, the oldest in the city, to the **Colegiata de Santa María del Sar**, one of the most interesting examples of the Romanesque style that gradually spread from France with the pilgrims along the *Camino* to Santiago. In view of the considerable historical-artistic-cultural-religious value of the mediaeval part of the city, in 1992 UNESCO proclaimed Santiago a heritage of humanity.

The elaborately sculpted and decorated Baroque façade of the Santiago de Compostela Cathedral, flanked by its soaring twin towers. Framed within an arch among the ornate spires of the towers, the statue of St. James (left) looks down and watches over the city.

HALTS ALONG THE ROUTE TO SANTIAGO

Since the IX century, thousands and thousands of pilgrims, blessed by the Church, start out on a very long journey that takes them from the East to the West of northern Spain to pay homage to the remains of James the Elder, the Apostle, which lie in the crypt of the **Santiago de Compostela Cathedral**.

Estella, ancient seat of the Navarra royal court, held in an austere palace, was one of the principal halts for pilgrims going to Santiago, who usually stayed in the Cistercian monastery of **N**

Astorga, which was a strategic settlement for the Romans along the important Silver Route, maintained this fundamental feature in connection with the Santiago Camino, becoming one of the main halts for pilgrims nearing their sacred destination.

León, the ancient capital of mozarabic Spain, still has monuments that relate of its centuries-old splendour, like the splendid Cathedral, magnificently adorned with huge stained-glass windows.

At **Burgos**, in the shadows of its Gothic Cathedral, everything is connected with pilgrims, even the famous

statue that synthesises all the historical symbols of a pilgrimage to Santiago: a walking stick, a pumpkin and scallop-shells.

Puente la Reina *takes its name from the pedestrian bridge that was built by royal order in the XI century to facilitate pilgrims crossing the River Arga.*

ñora de Irache.

á n t i c o

Pamplona, *capital of Navarra since the X century and famous today for the Fiesta de los Sanfermines as well, welcomed pilgrims after their climb over the Pyrenees to safety and shelter behind its solid walls and, from the XVI century onwards, inside the well-appointed fortress.*

Not far from Puente la Reina, in an isolated part of the countryside, the Romanesque church of **Santa María de Eunate** *offered travellers a brief but refreshing rest under the cool vaults of its external portico, but it was also the appointed place for burying pilgrims who had died along the Camino.*

BILBAO

SAN SEBASTIÁN

RONCESVALLES

PAMPLONA

PUENTE LA REINA

EUNATE

ESTELLA

JAVIER

LEYRE

BURGOS

SANTO DOMINGO DE LA CALZADA

SANGÜESA

N

The San Salvador de **Leyre** *Monastery, immersed in vegetation, for centuries was an important spiritual centre where the Cistercian monks, protected under patronage of the Kings of Navarra, toiled and led a life as austere as the architecture of their church and its underlying crypt.*

Javier *boasts a crenellated fortress where St. Francesco Saverio was born in the XVI century.*

GALICIAN FESTIVAL

The people of Galicia, of remote Celtic origin, have always lived an almost isolated existence, protected by the range of mountains which practically separates these lands from the rest of the Iberian Peninsula. This has led to Galicia having some unique characteristics, like the costumes and traditions, which are still jealously preserved and handed down from one generation to another. An example is the *gaita*, the typical Galician instrument similar to Scottish bagpipes. However, the local fiestas are the real source of pride of these areas; brightly coloured costumes and rhythmic folkdances enliven the main celebrations throughout the year and attract increasing numbers of tourists. Hence, Carnival is 'challenged' with particularly unusual masks, all types of tricks and breathtaking rhythms; Corpus Domini is celebrated with picturesque decorations, made with flower petals, and with solemn processions; street dancing and fireworks celebrate St. James' Day on 25th July. However, a very special event takes place between May and June and involves practically everyone in the various towns where it is held: this is the famous *Rapa das Bestas*, when the manes and tails of the beautiful Galician horses are trimmed.

Two views of Valladolid: above, the austere San Benito Church and, left, the modest little house where Miguel de Cervantes spent the last years of his adventurous life.

VALLADOLID

Valladolid, one of the historical Castile-León cities, which grew and developed under Arabian dominion but which was proclaimed capital of the kingdom in 1492 by Ferdinand and Isabella, the Catholic Monarchs who were actually married here in 1469, lived moments of particular splendour during the Renaissance, as the beautiful architecture and monuments testify. The churches of **San Pablo**, **San Benito**, and **Santa María la Antigua** stand out stately from the others, as well as the majestic, but never completed **Cathedral**, which was started in 1580 by Juan de Herrera, the favourite architect of Philip II, the king who was born in Valladolid. The sober, essential *interior* with its rows of mighty columns contrast the elegant, elaborate façade, embellished with intricate arabesques. Valladolid is famous for its XIV century **University**, a demonstration of the very keen cultural climate that has distinguished the city for centuries; but it is also famous because Christopher Columbus came here to die, in absolute solitude, and Miguel de Cervantes, the author of Don Quixote, spent his last years here.

LEÓN

Originally created by the Ancient Romans, made capital of the kingdom of Ordoño II during mediaeval times prior to being occupied by the Arabs, taken over by Christians at the turn of the XI century then capital of Spain for a short period and dynamic centre of the *Reconquista*, León still keeps the severe appearance of a mediaeval settlement with its intricate network of tiny, narrow streets and lanes. Its impressive **Cathedral** covers 1,800 m² of ground at the foot of the Cordillera Cantábrica from where it dominates the city, and its interior is illuminated by superb, polychromatic stained-glass windows: this natural illumination inside the church is what has made it famous, because almost 200 rose windows, all different in shape and size and all with differently aged decorations and subjects, create an extraordinary trick of light and hues.

The splendid, luminous León Cathedral, famous for its stained-glass windows. The soaring nave stretches upwards in a play of arches and buttresses.
Below, a view revealing some exquisite details of the Cathedral doorways surmounted by elegant, sculptured decorations dating back to the XIII century.

Started during the XIII century and finished in the following century, this enormous structure built along slender Gothic lines and in which the sepulchre of Ordoño II lies, has a remarkable, frescoed *cloister* attached to it which deserves a visit, as does the **Cathedral Museum,** where authentic works of art by Spanish artists from the Romanesque period onwards are exhibited. Another of the outstanding monuments that give lustre to the city and deserve particular mention is the **Colegiata de San Isidoro**, the beautiful basilica built to house the ashes of St. Isidoro of Seville, brought here to escape attack by the Moors.

Sober but noble elegance distinguishes the Colegiata de San Isidoro (above), the second most important monument in the city after the Cathedral. The tombs of the first sovereigns of León and Castile lie here in the Panteón Real, and the ashes of St. Isidoro of Seville were brought here for stately burial when the advancing Moors threatened the sacred remains. On the right, a detail of the group statue that sits over the Colegiata entrance door. On the opposite page, a hieratic bas-relief depicting St. Isidoro.

But the real gem of the collegiate church is inside it: the **Panteón Real**, an ancient mausoleum erected to provide appropriate graves for the first kings of León and Castile, more than twenty of whom rest under the austere vaults. The whole mausoleum is superbly decorated with XII century *frescoes* depicting bible scenes and moments of mediaeval life, and the capitals that support the vaulted roof are elegantly figured. The whole scene resembles an exquisite jewel box filled with precious pearls of mediaeval art.

Another interesting building is the **Hostal de San Marcos**, erected on the banks of the river Bernesga that runs through the city, and now partially taken up by a luxurious *parador*. It was built in the XII century as a hostel for pilgrims going to Santiago, then renovated and given its characteristic plateresque *façade* covered with shells when it became the seat of the Santiago Cavaliers, and at one point it was even transformed into a jailhouse for political prisoners.

During the XVIII century, the elegant Baroque *gable* was added on and the impressive, monumental construction is still admired today for its elegant *church* and *cloisters*, and for the adjacent **Museo Arqueológico Provincial**, which holds a precious XI century ivory crucifix known as the *Cristo de Carrizo*.

ASTORGA

Once a Roman settlement of considerable strategic importance, then a halt for pilgrims on their way to Santiago, Astorga is a pleasant city huddled at the feet of its ancient town, protected by sturdy ramparts. The majestic **Cathedral**, which took four centuries to build (XV to XVIII) and required the supervision of an enormous number of architects, stands right in the heart of the ancient district. However, the result is a superb, composite building displaying different styles, from Gothic to Baroque, all harmoniously combined in a spectacular synthesis. The adjacent **Museum** is famous for the treasures it conserves, the most precious of which is the *Reliquary of the Real Cross*, a goldsmith's work of art studded with many, many jewels. Right on front of the Cathedral, standing between two Baroque towers, there is another interesting construction: the **Palacio Episcopal** that Antoni Gaudí built in Gothic-revival style at the end of the XIX century in place of the previous palace, which was destroyed by fire in 1887. Gaudí's typical originality was fully expressed in this work, to the extent that he was so heavily criticised in ecclesiastic circles that the building was never used as an episcopal palace. It now houses an interesting *collection of sacred art*, particularly items from mediaeval Astorga.

Two views of the ancient centre of Astorga, showing (above) the elaborate Cathedral flanked by the enchanting Palacio Episcopal.

MEDINA DEL CAMPO

Medina del Campo owes its fame to its castle, built in 1440 with crenellated battlements and an impressive square tower, the so-called *Homenaje Tower* that was the impregnable residence of lord of the manor. When it became property of the Spanish royal family, this **Castillo de la Mota**, a classical example of *Mudéjar* style construction which used humble materials – bricks in this case –, was inhabited by King Ferdinand and Queen Isabella; Isabella died in Medina in 1504, but not in the *castillo* because it had been transformed into a prison by then.

TORDESILLAS

In Tordesillas – the town where Spain and Portugal signed a treaty for the partition of American territories in 1494 – stands the **Convento de Santa Clara**, an authentic piece of Andalusia within the Castile and León region: merit of this goes to María de Padilla, mistress of Pedro, son of Alphonse XI who ordered the convent to be built in the XIV century. María longed for her home country so much that she wanted the building covered all over with Moorish decorations. Perhaps these beautiful decorations consoled Joanna the Mad when, after the death of her husband, she retreated to the convent in 1509 and lived there for almost half a century in voluntary isolation.

The Castillo de la Mota, in Medina del Campo, and, right, Moorish decorations in one of the patios of the Convento de Santa Clara in Tordesillas.

SUNFLOWERS

The sunflower is an extremely decorative plant, with its large, dull green leaves and its bright yellow flowers with long petals circled round a heart of seeds. Originating in certain areas of the American continent (Mexico, Peru, Chile), sunflowers were imported to Europe during the XVI century by Spanish conquerors and immediately found their ideal habitat where the land was most fertile, deep and 'mellow'. At first, it was grown merely as an ornamental plant and it was not until later that it was appreciated for the oil its seeds produce and for its many other important, nutritional properties. This eventually led to its extensive culture, to the immense stretches of golden yellow that brighten the greenery of the countryside and have attracted and inspired so many poets and artists. In Spain, in particular, there are many occasions for admiring a fascinating natural scene like this: in Summer, the countryside around Burgos is full of enormous fields of sunflowers swaying in the breeze, with their heads stretched towards the sun; a scene which has no rival, except in the similar areas which brighten the Andalusian countryside.

BURGOS

History has always been part of the charming town of Burgos, for centuries famous for its profitable wool trade. Stretched out in a cradle of green plateaux, this was another of the important halts along the road to Santiago; it was capital of the Castile and León realms before Valladolid, and was the place where the Catholic Monarchs, Ferdinand and Isabella, met Christopher Columbus in the XV century **Casa del Cordón** on his return from his second voyage to the New World. In much more recent times, Francisco Franco established his headquarters here during the Civil War. However, this IX

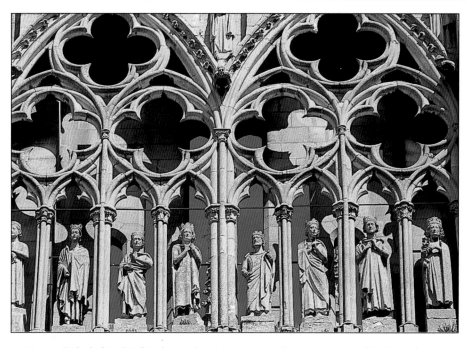

Burgos Cathedral (a detail is shown above) is an outstanding masterpiece of Gothic architecture.

century city, which was set up as a defence-post against the devastating advance of the Moors, is above all the home town of El Cid, whose presence practically pores out of every corner and whose statue guards the *Puente de San Pablo*, the most important of the city's bridges across the river Arlanzón.

Playing such a constant and important role in Spanish history over the years could only lead to Burgos having outstanding architecture. For instance, the massive *Arco de Santa María*, the solid, turreted gateway crowned with statues that opens the way to the old part of the town; and the **Iglesia de Santa Águeda**, the church where the newly crowned Alphonse VI swore to El Cid (whom he wanted in his entourage) that he had played no part in the murder of his brother, Sancho II; or the **Monasterio de las Huelgas Reales** (XII century), a Cistercian convent where only women from high society could become nuns and where its abbess allowed only the Queen of Spain to walk on front of her; besides holding the tombs of some of the first kings of Castile, the convent has a precious collection of cloths and jewels on display in the **Museo de Ricas Telas**. Moreover, just outside

Burgos, there is the XV century **Cartuja de Miraflores** with the graves of King Juan II and Isabella of Portugal, who were the parents of Isabella the Catholic, and of Don Alphonse, her brother who died young. Isabella actually encouraged the completion of the adiacent church because she wanted to give her relatives graves befitting their rank, and the sumptuous, radiant decorations that ornate these sepulchres definitely make them stand out.

However, the real source of pride in Burgos is undoubtedly the spectacular **Cathedral**, a magnificent work of art in which some of the most famous European architects have left their mark throughout the centuries. Begun in 1221, this slender Gothic church, so distinctly opulent, gradually became a mausoleum to El Cid, who is buried here in the centre of the transept together with his wife, Ximena.

The Cathedral, with its many pointed spires, was finished only in the XVI century when the splendid central *dome* was erected, and owes its fame not only to the richly adorned chapels – the *Capilla del Condestable*, the chapel

The Virgin with Child *watches over Burgos from the top of the Cathedral.*

An original statue stands out in one the squares in Burgos: a pilgrim sits resting on his way to Santiago.

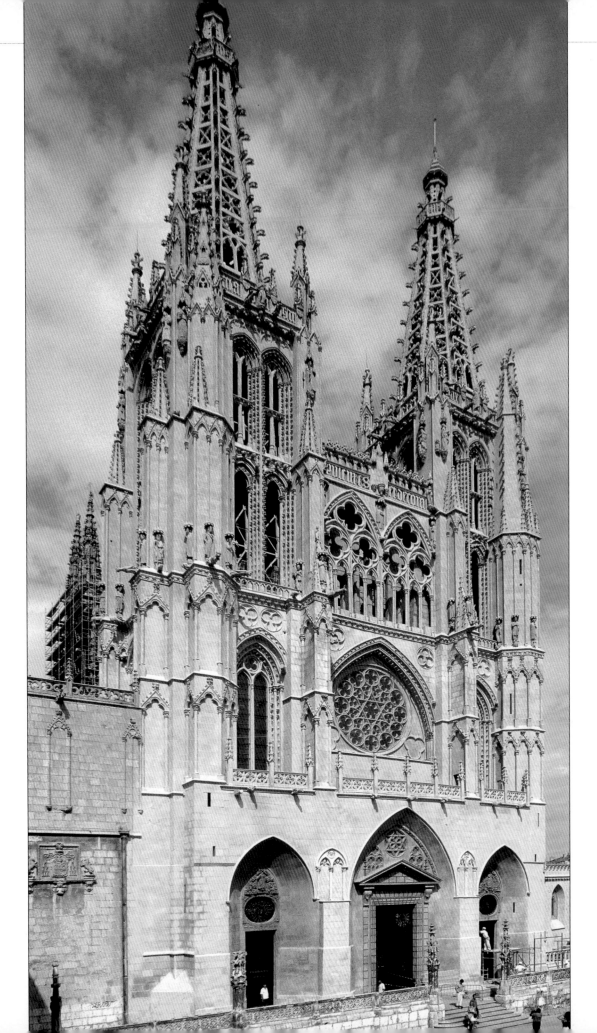

El Cid Campeador

Rodrigo Díaz was born in 1043 into a noble family in Vivar, near Burgos, and was brought up at the court of Sancho II, King of Castile, to whom he became a valiant lieutenant. However, when Sancho was murdered in 1072, he served under his brother who was crowned Alphonse VI and who took him into service only after assuring that he nothing to do with the crime. He fell into disgrace and, ex-iled from the Castile court in 1081, went back to Burgos with his wife, Ximena, a cousin of the king. He then offered his services first to the Moorish king of Saragozza, then to the king of Valencia; the Muslim soldiers gave him the Arabi-an title of *Sid* (master) which became *Cid* and was coupled with the nickname he already had, *Campeador*, 'the battle-winner'. Forever loyal, he never wanted to fight against his 'own' king and in 1094 he reconquered Valencia for the Christians and remained there as ruler until his death in 1099. His wife brought the hero's body back to Burgos in 1102, to bury him in the Cathedral; this authentic paladin of the *Reconquista* was immortalised in the epic poem, *El Cantar del mio Cid*.

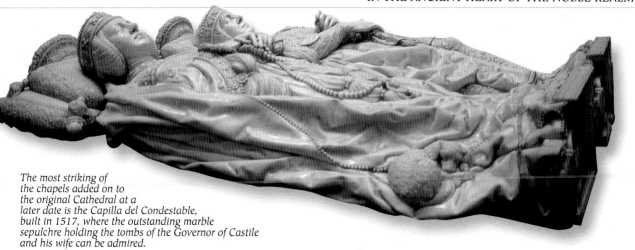

The most striking of
the chapels added on to
the original Cathedral at a
later date is the Capilla del Condestable,
built in 1517, where the outstanding marble
sepulchre holding the tombs of the Governor of Castile
and his wife can be admired.

holding the sepulchres of the Governor of Castile and his wife (1517), the *Capilla de Santa Ana* with its beautiful alter-piece by Gil de Siloé (1490), to mention just two – or to the elegant, graceful *cloisters*, or the *Escalera Dorada*, designed by Diego de Siloé in the XVI century, but also to a curious statue: an extremely unusual life-size *statue of Christ*, with human hair on the head and buffalo skin clothes.

Nevertheless, tourists who are attracted to Burgos by its architectural monuments and its historical past can also discover other things typical of the city, like its delicious bean stew or roast lamb which are the best in the whole of Spain. These healthy, substantial dishes are naturally more enjoyable in Winter, because winters in Burgos are very cold, just as they are in many areas of the vast *meseta*.

A view of the luminous interior of the Cathedral. Particularly worth noting, are the lavish decorations and the upward soar of the high Gothic vaults; while daylight filters and flickers through the stained-glass windows.

79

ZAMORA

Situated not far from the Portuguese border, the ancient town of Zamora has always served as a strategic site since Roman times, and because of this, it was often heatedly contended. This explains the presence of the well-appointed, fortified *city walls*

surrounding Zamora and which are now over a thousand years old, since Alphonse III had them built at the end of the IX century; some very significant parts of these walls still stand, like the famous *'Traitor's Gateway'*, where King Sancho II was treacherously murdered in the XI century. However, there are other splendid monuments which narrate of Zamora's glorious past: in particular, there are several austere *Romanesque Churches* (like those dedicated to St. Idelfonso and to Mary Magdalene, both of which have intricately carved *doorways*) and what is known as *'El Cid's House'*,

because the hero is believed to have been knighted here in the church dedicated to *Santiago de los Caballeros*. But the real jewel in Zamora is definitely the **Cathedral**, which was planned along Romanesque lines in the XII century and finished with Gothic features; then, later still, a Byzantine semi-spherical dome surrounded by a circlet of turrets and covered with characteristics scales was added on. Worth seeing inside are the magnificent XV century *choir-stalls*, the carved seats of which depict very vivid scenes of monastery life, actually rather daring scenes considering the period. The adjacent **museum** holds a rich collection of beautifully designed Flemish tapestries from the XV century. Another interesting **museum** is the one called **'de la Semana Santa'** (of the Holy Week) that all year round exhibits the *pasos*, the enormous allegorical floats which are taken through the city streets during the Holy Week processions.

Above: the Cathedral; left: a splendid detail of Magdalen Church; right: the Casa del Cordón, one of the most beautiful buildings in Zamora and where storks still make their nests.

SALAMANCA

Salamanca owes its fortune to the fact that it lies in the centre of what was once called the 'Silver Route', the road which connected the mines in southern Spain with the busy ports facing the Atlantic Ocean. Therefore, at one point during its over two thousand years of history, Salamanca was an important and strategic Roman settlement, and was also the place farthest West conquered by Hannibal. After being occupied by the Moors for a long time, it returned definitely to Christian hands in 1085 and took its first steps towards its glorious future: in 1218, Alphonse IX established one of the most important universities in Europe here, the **University** of Salamanca, which is in one of the finest examples of Castilian architecture, an elegant building with a plateresque façade dominated by

The medallion with images of the Catholic Monarchs, in the centre of the main façade of Salamanca University.

images of the Catholic Monarchs and an overwhelming abundance of arabesques and decorations; the university also contains a very well stocked **Library** dating back to the XVIII century and containing over 50,000 volumes, incunabula and manuscripts. However, Salamanca is famous as being the city with two **Cathedrals**. The first of these, now known as the **Old Cathedral**, was started in 1150 with donations from private citizens, and was built to celebrate the city being freed from the Moors by King Alphonse VI after centuries of struggle, fighting, siege and devastation. The building is subdued and austere, as befits a strictly Romanesque creation, though it already had some features pointing towards the future Gothic style, like the tall, slender bundle columns that flank the naves and the presence of ogive arches. Inside there are numerous *sarcophagi* and *sepul-*

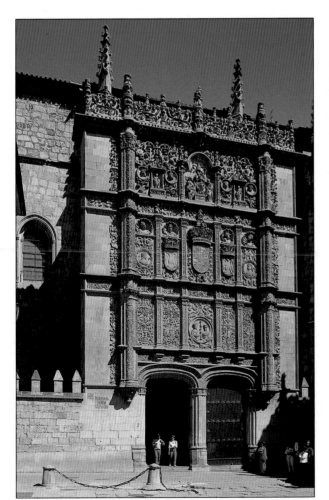

Plaza Mayor, built for Philip V and designed by the Churriguera brothers in 1729, is one of the most imposing squares in the whole of Spain.

The extremely elaborate XVI century façade of the University looking onto the Patio de las Escuelas Menores.

A detail of the Casa de las Conchas, decorated (as the name indicates) with 365 stone sea-shells.

chres, often fitted into niches or in little chapels, and above all, there is a splendid, gigantic Gothic **retable** against the curved wall of the apsis: made of 53 panels dated 1445 and depicting episodes of the New Testament, this was the work of two Italian artists who were then working in Spain, the Florentine Dello Delli and his brother Nicolás, better known as Nicolás Fiorentino and author of the *Last Judgement* as well, which dominates the altar-frontal from the apsis basin. The *cloisters* built next to the church in the same century were given neo-classic features in the XVIII century, after being damaged by the same earthquake that destroyed Lisbon in 1755. However, by the XVI century the size of the Cathedral was considered inadequate for the city, which had begun attracting famous people like Christopher Columbus, Cer-

vantes, St. Thérèse and Hernán Cortés because of its university and its cultural atmosphere. Therefore, instead of enlarging the existing basilica, a new, bigger and more majestic one was planned beside it: the **New Cathedral**. However, this was not merely built *next* to the older one; it actually merged *into* part of its northern nave with its southern walls. On the other hand, even though work had started in the middle of the Renaissance, in 1512, the new building respected the older one in an incredibly philological manner and was erected in what was, by then, an out of date Gothic style, with imposing ribbed pillars which are larger versions of the bundle pillars in the Old Cathedral, and with wide, four-light windows through which daylight filters in abundance to illuminate the high naves filled with solemnity. The first stage of the work finished in 1568; the second stage, however, took until 1733 and this meant that even Late-Gothic and Baroque styles were to leave their mark in this New Cathedral: Late-Gothic, the Gothic that went down in history as 'Hispanic-Flamenco', is in fact the style of the very elaborate *façade*, designed by Juan Gil de Hontañón and finished in 1538 with a triumph of inlay work and relief sculptures around the magnificent *Nativity Door*; Baroque is the style of the statues, like the organ, the windows, the *choir-stall* designed in 1724 by Joaquín Churriguera, and above all, the cross *dome*, which was also damaged in the 1755 earthquake. The outcome

The unmistakable mass of the New Cathedral, beside the Old Cathedral, dominates Salamanca from high above and reflects in the waters of River Tormes, which is crossed by the ancient Puente Romano as well as other more recent bridges.

The spectacular Nativity Door, which opens into the New Cathedral.

The enormous retable that embellishes the apsis of the Old Cathedral: made of 53 framed panels, painted by the Florentine artists Dello Delli and his brother Nicolás, this masterpiece is one of the most significant examples of Gothic art in XV century Spain.

is therefore a mixture of many different styles and elements, producing an incredibly harmonious effect as the monument reflects in the waters of the river Tormes. All around it, an elegant, vivacious city with many interesting spots: like the fine **Puente Romano** which bridges the river at the bottom of Salamanca, and the **Escuelas Menores**, beyond an elegant *patio* in the XVI Dominican convent, **San Esteban**, a plateresque-style work of art which is believed to have accommodated even Christopher Co-

The XIII sepulchre of Alfonso Vidal in the Old Cathedral.

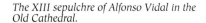

lumbus; or the **Casa de las Conchas**, a noble palace not far from the Plaza Mayor, decorated with 365 stone shells and enhanced with magnificent, lavishly decorated cloisters of Moorish inspiration. And all along the streets, throngs of *tunas*, students who follow the typical goliardic traditions of the University, roaming the streets in mediaeval costume with coloured hose and singing ancient melodies to the accompaniment of modern guitars.

Salamanca in one of the famous scenes reproduced on ceramic tiles in the Plaza de España, Seville.

SEGOVIA

Perched high up on a rock, splendid Segovia has been silhouetted against a backdrop of bright blue skies for thousands of years, from the 1st century AD, in fact, when the Romans began using this naturally strategic defence-post as an impregnable military base. Trace of that period in the city remains to this day: the striking **aqueduct** (I-II centuries AD) with two rows of arches, almost 30 metres high and over 700 metres long, erected to supply the town with water from the Río Frío filtered through a series of tanks, but now literally smothered by houses. On the opposite side of Segovia, towards West, there is another of the city's emblems, the fairy-tale **Alcázar** with its array of battlements and turrets, now the site of an interesting **Weapon Museum**. Built in the XII century and restored during the XV century, the ori-

The Roman aqueduct, with its sturdy arches, is one of the most famous monuments in Segovia, and has now been englobed almost entirely by the structures of this modern city.

ginal Alcázar was destroyed by fire and thereafter completely rebuilt in 1862; this was when it was given the ethereal form we see today. And in between these two very different monuments sits Segovia's third gem, the splendid Gothic **Cathedral** capped with spires, turrets and an elegant dome, and with its adjacent, imposing bell-tower. Started in 1525 and finished in 1678, the Cathedral stands on the site of a previous one, destroyed during the Castile territory rebellion in 1520: only the cloisters of the former building were saved. So, in this city that Isabella the Catholic loved, the place where she was crowned, the heart of the ferocious *Inquisition*, the birth-place or favourite residence of artists and writers, like Antonio Machado the famous poet, in the city that the Bourbons aroused from the serious economical and cultural depression that set in at the beginning of the XVII century, many other beautiful works of art risk being shadowed under the glow of these impor-

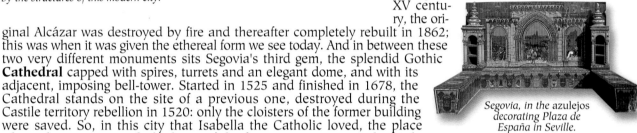

Segovia, in the azulejos decorating Plaza de España in Seville.

tant monuments: for example, the **Casa de los Picos**, a XVI century palace with a diamond-point ashlar façade, or the **Romanesque Church of San Martín**, facing onto the square with the *monument dedicated to Juan Bravo*, the hero who led Segovia's unsuccessful struggle against the armies of Charles V.

On the following pages: the slender contours of the Gothic Cathedral, enhanced by numerous spires.

On page 88: the fantastic Alcázar, entirely reconstructed during the XIX century.

ÁVILA

The ancient city of Ávila, which legends maintain founded by Hercules and which is famous for its great and beautifully preserved mediaeval **walls**, stands high and secure at over 1,100 metres above sea level, where the climate in Winter can be particularly harsh; the XI century walls are over 2.5 km long, over 3 metres thick and 12 metres high, with 88 turrets at regular intervals and nine gateways, and are particularly attractive to storks who often make their nests on the top. Another of the city's monuments is the stunning Gothic **Cathedral** with its unusual, military air (the apsis actually appears englobed within the city walls). Above all, Ávila is famous for the fact that the great mystical reformer of the Carmelite Order destined to become **St. Theresa**, Teresa de Cepeda y Ahumada, was born into a noble family there in 1515. She vehemently preached the virtues of poverty and tirelessly went all around Spain founding numerous convents. Her grave is not far from Salamanca,

St. Theresa was born in Ávila and spent her youth within its striking mediaeval walls; the statue on the right, which dominates the façade of the church in Palermo that bears her name, demonstrates that she is worshipped by faithful followers throughout the whole world.

but the magnificence of her work has left its indelible mark in Ávila, her home town, where everything seems to speak of her: the **Convento de Santa Teresa** built on the spot of her birthplace, the **Monasterio de la Encarnación** where she lived for over 20 years and where her cell can still be seen, and the **Real Monasterio de Santo Tomás** that holds the sepulchre of Prince Juan, the only son of Ferdinand and Isabella, the Catholic Monarchs who founded the monastery.

The mighty mediaeval walls, with 88 turrets at regular intervals, still surround Ávila and give it its particular appearance.

THE MESETA

Meseta is the term used to describe the vast plateau in the
Old and New Castile regions in the heart of the Iberian
Peninsula, divided down the centre by a backbone of
mountain ranges rich in woodlands (Sierra de
Guadarrama, Sierra de Gredos, Sierra de Gata).
Composed of granitic rock upon which the layers of
deposited sediment are insufficient for thick vegetation,
these areas where the climate is substantially Continental
appear more or less like enormous stretches of steppe,
scattered here and there with thickets and furrowed by
many rivers. In the Old Castile region, these plateaux can
be as high as 1,000 metres above sea level and are rarely
lower than 700 metres: in New Castile, the plateaux are
not so high. In spite of this, the inhabitants have managed
to get the most out of the limited resources of the area by
creating extensive cultures of cereals: wheat in the
western parts of the *meseta* where the land is more fertile
and irrigation is better, and barley, mainly in the South
where the climate is drier.

To really get to know Madrid, the starting point is necessarily its historical centre: that **Plaza Mayor**, closed within elegant buildings built over porticoes, which was the first serious work performed by the Hapsburgs twenty years or so after the start of the XVII century in what had been, until then, a somewhat mediocre urban system in the new capital, even though the original idea had really been one of Philip II and his devoted architect, Juan de Herrera. The outcome was a fully paved square measuring over 16,000 m², capable of holding more than one third of what was then the population in Madrid. For a long time, public ceremonies were held here, as well as the Inquisition court sessions and the infliction of capital punishment; bull fights were performed here, as well – and on these occasions the balconies and windows were rented out –; but there were also three devastating fires here. This is why the present-day appearance of the square traces back no farther than 1790, having been designed by the architect called Juan de Villanueva. The centre of the square is dominated by a *statue of Philip III on horseback*, started by Giambologna and finished by Pietro Tacca around 1613. There are delightful open-air cafés and many interesting buildings all around the square, like the XVI century *Casa de la Panadería*, recently frescoed by Carlos Franco, and the *Casa de la Carnicería*, connected with the historical guilds of bakers and butchers, respectively.

Views of Madrid: the historical centre of the city – the spectacular Plaza Mayor –; the equestrian statue of Philip III that dominates the centre of the square; and Madrid's emblem, the great bear eating fruit from an arbutus tree, part of the city's coat of arms and seen here in bronze in a corner of Puerta del Sol.

MADRID

The origins of Madrid are lost in ancient times and are historically uncertain: even the actual meaning of the city's name remains a mystery, it might come from *magerit*, the Arabian word meaning 'great bridge'. For many centuries after being conquered by the Romans, Madrid was just a small agricultural settlement where the inhabitants also bred cattle, 660 metres above sea level in the heart of the *meseta*. The first stronghold originated when the Arabs conquered it in the IX century; then Alphonse VI of Castile returned it to Christianity in 1080. Following this latter event, life in Madrid was uneventful until King Philip II, engrossed in erecting the stupendous Escorial on the nearby Sierra de Guadarrama, changed both the history and the appearance of the city: in 1561, all of a sudden tiny Madrid became the capital of the kingdom, the centre for his court and the entire aristocracy, and the government; the population increased enormously; the city started expanding, especially towards Northeast, and was embellished with imposing monuments. By the XVIII century, therefore, when the Bourbons took over from the Hapsburgs of Spain, the lineage that ended with Charles III, the densely populated agricultural town had already become a political and cultural centre of primary importance. The new dynasty incremented the city's splendour even further, by adding on new palaces, avenues and beautiful parks. In spite of various difficult political, economical and demographical moments, Madrid continued to develop and pave the way for the city as we see it today, a very lively metropolis with almost four million inhabitants who now savour re-birth and renewal following the return of democracy.

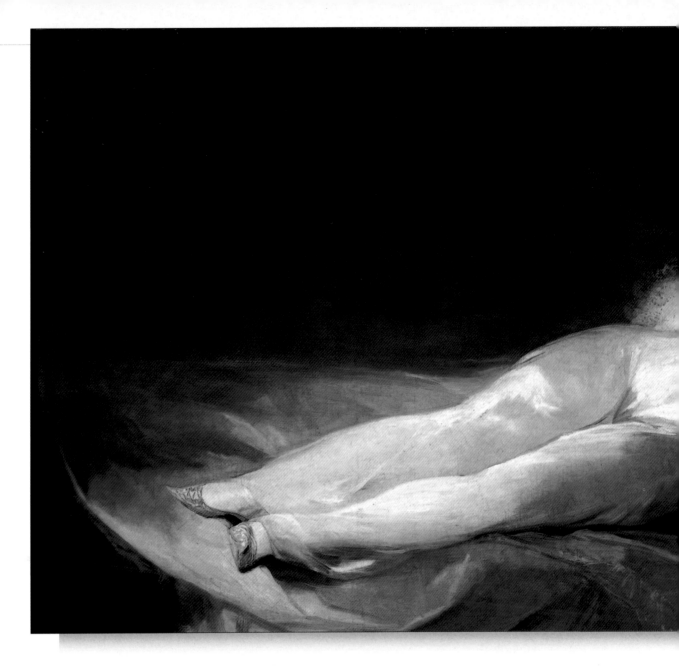

Perfectly at its ease now as Capital City, Madrid boasts cultural institutions of worldwide importance, like the **Prado Museum**, a real treasure chest of art. In the second half of the XVIII century, Charles III, one of the sovereigns who had striven most to free the city of the provincial air left by its modest origins, entrusted the skilled architect Juan de Villaneuva with the task of remodelling the *Prado de San Gerolamo* attached to the monastery bearing the same name, to create botanical gardens complete with an astronomical observatory and a museum, which originally was supposed to exhibit only the natural science specimens belonging to the monarchy. However, after the devastating napoleonic wars, the project was enlarged and became more ambitious: in 1819 therefore, to celebrate the arrival in Madrid of Maria Giuseppina Amelia the Saxon, third wife of King Ferdinand VII, a magnificent museum complex was officially opened beyond the elegant, neo-classical *Velázquez Door*, surrounded by imposing Doric columns. The priceless royal collection of paintings, source of pride and emblem of an

extraordinarily powerful and illustrious dynasty, finds an appropriate setting here: thousands of paintings collected by different sovereigns throughout the centuries, plus many other works of art accumulated during the following decades, resulting in the greatest collection of Spanish paintings in the world (ranging from the XII to the XIX century). Nowadays, the over 7,000 paintings, 4,000 drawings and approximately 900 sculptures (500 of which are from the Classic period) can be exhibited in the 80 rooms only by means of rotating them in series, because there is space for no more than 1,300 items at a time. It is therefore quite difficult to give an adequate account of the historical and artistic treasures kept in the Prado: the *Spanish School* section has works by José de Ribera, El Greco (a whole collection), Francisco de Zurbarán, and by Diego Velázquez and Francisco Goya, the court painters; the *Flemish and Dutch School* section – it must be remembered that the Netherlands were under Spanish dominion for a long time, just like large areas of Italy – exhibits paintings by Van der Weyden,

Two particularly famous masterpieces by Francisco Goya hang among other important Spanish paintings in the Prado: the Maja vestida and the Maja desnuda, painted between 1797 and 1805. In these two paintings, the same young lady, in the same pose, is seen first dressed in eastern-style finery, and then completely naked in the second. This was the artist's extremely personal way of dealing with the tricky question of nudity. A method which caused a great amount of controversy at the time, besides clear accusations of obscenity.

In the section dedicated to Flemish School paintings, a painting worth mentioning because of the drama, gloom and pathos that emerge with violence from the particularly intense colours, is the Triumph of Death, a XVI century masterpiece by Brueghel the Elder: here, the artist drew inspiration from the massacres that were one of the worst consequences of Spanish domination in the Netherlands.

Brueghel the Elder, Bosch – one of King Philip II's favourite artists – and about one hundred paintings by Rubens, as well as two masterpieces by Rembrandt; the *Italian School* is well represented with works of art by Botticelli, Raffaello, Veronese, Titian, Caravaggio and Tiepolo, and above all the delightful *Annunciation* by Beato Angelico dating back to 1430; the *French and German Schools* are also significantly portrayed through works like those of Poussin, Van Loo and Watteau, and Dürer, Mengs and Cranach.

Not very far from the museum, on the hill where the historical *Parque del Retiro* is situated, stands the **Casón del Buen Retiro** which was already intended as a separate part of the Prado in the original plans: here there are many interesting paintings and sculptures on show, but all from the end of the XIX century to the beginning of the XX century. For a short time, the Prado also held the magnificent Picasso masterpiece, *Guernica*, which the artist had brought back from New York in 1981 after democracy was restored to Spain. However, this was transferred in 1992 to the ultra modern **Centro de Arte Reina Sofía**, opened up in the antique Madrid General Hospital, appropriately remodelled to house a four-storey gallery exhibiting exclusively XX century art.

One of the many Velázquez paintings in the Prado is a very unusual one. When visitors look at Las Meniñas (or The Maids-of-Honour, painted around 1656), they are actually looking at it from the same view-point as the two sovereigns, Philip IV and his wife Anna Maria, who were posing for the artist and can been seen reflected in the mirror. And the artist painted himself in the group as well: he can be seen standing next to the perky Infanta Margarita, surrounded by her maids-of-honour – doña Maria Agustina de Sarmiento and doña Isabel de Velasco –, but he also included the court dwarves, Mari Bárbola and Nicolasito Pertusato, then doña Marcela de Ulloa, standing behind with don Diego Ruiz de Azcona, and don José Nieto Velázquez in the background. Practically a photograph of the Spanish Court at that time.

The elegant Portrait of Charles V on horseback, *painted by Titian in 1548, is one of the most important pieces in the section dedicated to Italian artists in the Prado. The Emperor appears superb and determined, a stance befitting the triumphant victor of the heroic battle of Mühlberg, fought in Saxony in April 1547.*

If the Plaza Mayor is considered the historical centre of old Madrid, then **Plaza de España** is definitely the focal point of the modern capital. There were military barracks here once, for the soldiers who guarded the Royal Palace. Nowadays, it still has the appearance it was given during the Francoist regime: the 1948 *Edificio de España*, 23 storeys and 117 metres high, and the *Torre de Madrid*, better known as *La Jirafa* (35 storeys, 124 metres high, built between 1954 and 1959), both look down on the *monument to Miguel de Cervantes* by Lorenzo Coullaut-Valera (1928).

On front of the author's statue, at the bottom of an enormous obelisk, his most famous characters, Don Quixote and Sancho Panza, ride their tired horses. Sitting on the left is Dulcinea, the lady Don Quixote loved.

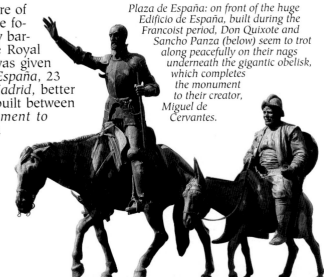

Plaza de España: on front of the huge Edificio de España, built during the Francoist period, Don Quixote and Sancho Panza (below) seem to trot along peacefully on their nags underneath the gigantic obelisk, which completes the monument to their creator, Miguel de Cervantes.

The Parque del Retiro, a beautiful, peaceful oasis in the heart of Madrid. Above, the monument to Alphonse XII that dominates the crystal-clear waters of the tiny lake.

One of the most pleasant parts of Madrid is the verdant **Parque del Retiro**, the largest public park in the city, a real oasis of peace that nevertheless boasts its own centuries of fame. It was originally created as a royal park for Philip IV in 1630 and was called the *Real Sitio del Buen Retiro*; its 120 hectares of lawns and woods, ponds and waterfalls once hosted lavish parties: naval battles were staged on its lake, theatrical events took place in the big arena known as the *Coliseo*, fabulous receptions were given on its shaded lawns to celebrate coronations, weddings and royal births. Then Charles III decided to open it up to the Madrilenians in 1767, the first step towards transforming the *Buen Retiro* into a public garden, or *parque municipal*, as it was proclaimed in 1868. There are also some interesting buildings amongst its greenery, like the *Casón del Buen Retiro*, now an art gallery, or the *Exhibition Palace*, a red brick building erected in 1887 and designed by Ricardo Velázquez Bosco, the architect who also designed the contemporary, Liberty-style *Palacio de Cristal*. On the banks of the lake, a favourite spot for oarsmen, stands the majestic *monument to Alphonse XII*, a crescent of classic columns topped with a balustrade and with a bronze *statue* of the king poised on a spectacular base in the foreground. All around there is the romantic, dreamy atmosphere of a place where time seems to stand still.

However, for the capital of any kingdom to be considered a real capital, it must have a flamboyant Royal Palace, and Madrid was no exception. Therefore, after yet another disastrous fire in 1734 had gutted the ancient *Alcázar*, the great royal stronghold at the western end of the old city, the reigning dynasty took advantage of the situation and built the new, magnificent **Royal Palace** in its place. And to accomplish this feat, the three kings who reigned throughout the work – Philip V, Ferdinand VI and Charles III – spent extravagant sums: it had to be gigantic, its opulence had to be unequalled. In 1755, four hundred men were still working on it and many million *pesetas* had already been spent on the huge construction. In 1755, the famous architect of the House of Savoy, Filippo Juvarra, was called to draw up the designs; he started immediately but died the following year. One of his promising scholars, Giovan Battista Sacchetti, took over but because of the expenses involved he had to re-design some parts of the plans drawn up by his Maestro. A beautiful park known as the *Campo del Moro* was created all round the building right down to the banks of the river Manzanares, and the white outlines of the palace stand out in striking contrast against the bright greenery; this creation was partly due to work performed subsequently by

Charles III's architect, Francesco Sabatini, who had previously worked with Vanvitelli on the Caserta Palace in Italy. Much attention was given to the interiors as well, engaging skilled artists like Giambattista Tiepolo, who was called first of all to fresco the ceiling in the *Throne Room* (*The Fame and Power of the Spanish Dynasty*, 1764), then to decorate the ceilings in the *Guard Room* and the *Queen's Boudoir*. Half way through the XVIII century, Corrado Giaquinto, the famous Neapolitan artist, was commissioned to paint the ceilings in the *Royal Chapel* and in the *Column Room*; this room has been used often during the latter part of the XX century as the venue for international political events, such as the official ceremony proclaiming Spain part of the European Economic Community in 1985, or the Middle East Peace Conference in 1991; however, the royal family has not lived here since 1931, but in Zarzuela, not far from Madrid.

The immense *Palacio Real* also houses two very interesting *museums*: the **Royal Pharmacy** with the famous Baroque *Herbarium* and an incredible collection of ceramic jars; and the **Royal Armoury**, an extraordinary collection of weapons, which gives its name to the large square on front of the palace entrance and its monumental *hallway* holding Sabatini's marble staircase: *Plaza de la Armería*.

The magnificent Royal Palace in Madrid, the elegance and splendour of which fulfilled all expectations of sovereigns who patronised its construction.

The Royal Palace seen from the beautiful park known as the Campo del Moro, and three views of its sumptuous interiors: left to right, Sabatini's monumental staircase, the Throne Room and the Hall of Mirrors.

A stunning view of the great Escorial, with the superb, imposing Basilica in the centre.

El Escorial

The *Sierra de Guadarrama*, which stretches out Northwest of Madrid City, is an impressive range of mountains where extremely cold winters with abundant snowfalls on its slopes have given rise to many excellent skiing resorts over the past decades. Right at the foot of the Sierra stands one of the most breathtaking examples of Spanish architecture ever seen, and which became the archetype of an extremely austere and particular style for many years: the noble **El Escorial** complex.

On the 10th August 1557, the feast day of St. Lawrence, the Spanish troops under Philip II won

an important battle over the French army in France. Being very religious, and to show his gratitude, in 1561 the king ordered a monastery to be built and dedicated to this saint at the foot of the Sierra de Guadarrama, to house monks of the Order of St. Jerome, and he decreed the immediate removal of the capital and his court to this sacred spot in the small city of Madrid. The project was commissioned to Juan Bautista de Toledo, who started work in Spring 1563 on the building that was to be finished only in 1586, long after his death in 1567; his work was taken over by Juan de Herrera who was already the Superintendent of Arts to the Crown. Herrera promptly engaged the best painters and sculptors of

One of the most praised parts of the beautiful monastery of San Lorenzo el Real in the Escorial – the name derives from the fact that it was built over the place used as a deposit for dross (scoriae) in the XVI century – is definitely the monumental Library, where visitors can admire the thousands of volumes enthusiastically collected by Philip II, the sovereign who ordered the construction of the convent. The bookcases and reading desks are, on their own, real masterpieces of elegant inlay work in precious wood. The ceilings are lavishly frescoed by the XVI artist Tibaldi, who described the world of Art and Science through a series of outstanding, spectacular allegorical figures.

that moment – like Benvenuto Cellini, El Greco, Jacopo da Trezzo and Luca Giordano – to guarantee the building with appropriately lavish decorations. And the results definitely fulfilled all expectations. Im-

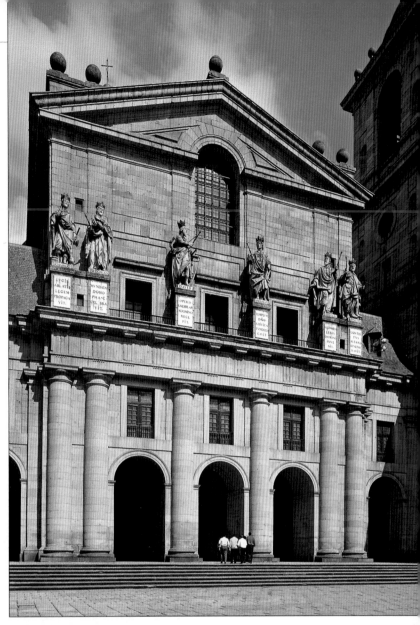

The severe façade of the Escorial Basilica, embellished with six impressive statues of biblical characters: Jehoshaphat, Ezekiel, David, Solomon, Joshua and Manasseh (top left is a detail of this last statue).

mersed in green woodland, the immense square and strictly symmetrical construction, guarded by a tower at all four corners, has not only a *monastery* but also a large **basilica** which, besides having a fine *altar-piece,* also includes the **Royal Pantheon**, a solemn mausoleum containing the tombs of Spanish sovereigns; Philip II's stately **Royal Chambers** leading directly into the basilica; the magnificent **Library** which holds a priceless treasure – the thousands of volumes collected by Philip II himself, including the very first poem in Castile language, written by Alphonse X –, as well as many precious decorations like the XVI century frescoes by Tibaldi that look down on the bookcases made of rare wood; and the more recent addition, an **Art Gallery** that displays Flemish paintings from Spain and Italy. Nevertheless, the interiors, the **Chapter Rooms** and even the many courtyards, all glow with magnificence and contrast beautifully with the severe and linear exterior. Since 1885, the fine complex has housed monks of the Order of St. Augustine and most parts of the building can be visited.

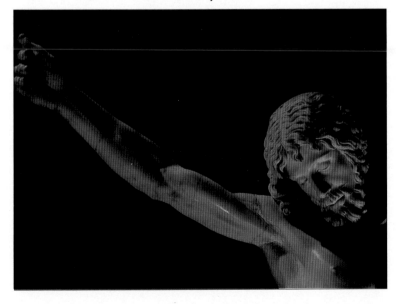

The Crucified Christ *by Benvenuto Cellini (1562), an exquisite work of art in marble given to Philip II by the Duke of Florence, on view inside the Basilica.*

TOLEDO

Still protected behind its ancient walls with nine gates, reached by a fine Roman bridge, the **Puente de Alcántara**, watched over by the **Castillo de San Servando**, Toledo has always played a foremost role throughout the different stages of history in the Iberian Peninsula, having been inhabited by the Romans – who built a fortress on the hill dominating the River Tagus – by Visigoths, Moors (who occupied the city in 711), Christians (after Alphonse VI took it over in 1085) and Jews. It was the Jews, in fact, who contributed greatly to the economical and artistic splendour of Toledo, during all the years they were able to live freely in the flourishing city: evidence of this is seen in the eight beautiful synagogues that adorned the city with their elegant architecture, two of which still stand out: the ancient *Sinagoga de Santa María* and the famous *Sinagoga del Tránsito*.
Capital of the kingdom for a long time, frequently but unsuccessfully besieged by the Arabs, Toledo lived for centuries in the productive atmosphere of wide-spread and tolerant cosmopolitanism, at least until the end of the XV century, when the Jews were expelled following a period of veiled crises resulting in considerable bloodshed.

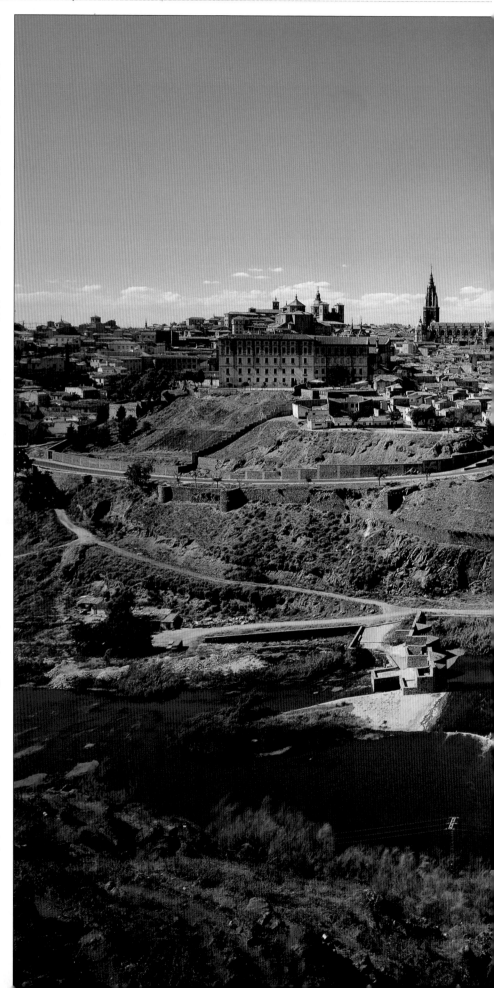

A fascinating panorama of Toledo nestling in a wide bend of the River Tago and dominated by both the magnificent Cathedral and the enormous Arabian fortress, which was transformed into a flamboyant palace for King Charles V during the XVI century.

Embraced in the crook of a wide bend in the River Tago, which furrows a little gorge at the foot of the city, protected on the other side by sturdy ramparts and with its Old City already a national monument, superb Toledo has been proclaimed by UNESCO one of the World's inestimable cultural treasures.

The Alcázar keeps guard over the Alcántara bridge and its tower looms over one end of it. A modern Monument to Victory stands outside the historical building (above). Inside, there is a stunning monumental stairway.

However, after Philip II had decided to transfer the capital to Madrid in 1561, Toledo slowly and relentlessly declined. Nevertheless, the majestic emblems of Toledo's previous splendour and rank as capital can still be seen dominating the city below: the striking Alcázar, for example, the Arabian fortress built over an ancient Roman stronghold that had defended the tiny *Toletum* and had been reconstructed several times. After accommodating the legendary *El Cid Campeador* who was made governor of the city by Alphonse VI, it became the official residence of Charles V, who entrusted the architect Alonso de Covarrubias with further work on the already huge, square fortress. A statue of this sovereign stands in the central patio of the fortress: Charles V is depicted with weapons drawn, towering over a defeated infidel. During the following centuries, the Alcázar went through ransack and destruction (the invasion of Napoleon's troops was particularly devastating), at least three fires, and from 1772 it was the headquarters of a charity organisation – the *Real Casa de la Caridad* – but was

The main façade of the Cathedral, started in 1418, looking on to the Municipal Square. The central entrance, known as the Puerta del Perdón (Pardon Door), adorned with statues of Saints, is opened only for special occasions (visits from Heads of State, investiture of a new Bishop) and grants indulgence on those who pass through.

almost completely destroyed in 1931 when a group of nationalists, led by José Moscardó Ituarte, commanding officer of the Toledo Military Academy that had its headquarters actually in the Alcázar, barricaded themselves inside the fortress during the Civil War and resisted a siege for many months. This episode is well documented inside the building and is acknowledged outside by means of a fine monument. Following this, the devastated Alcázar was beautifully reconstructed with philological competence and today, splendid as ever, houses an interesting military museum. However, the ancient centre of Toledo has yet another incomparable monument, the exquisite **Cathedral**, which was built in 1226 on the spot of a previous church and destined to be the see of the primate archbishop of Spain. Legends narrate of this being the spot where there had been an ancient chapel dedicated to St. Ildelfonso, the Patron Saint of the city, to whom the Madonna appeared, to reward him for his zealous battle against those who doubted Her virginity. After the invasion of the Moors, it was transformed into a mosque, then once more converted into a Christian church in 1085 by Alphonse V on his triumphant arrival in Toledo. However, this is legend. History shows that the new Cathedral was conceived with slender Gothic lines, dominated by a soaring tower, and since its construction continued until the turn of the XVI century, it inevitably ended up by being a mixture of different styles, such as Plateresque, Renaissance and Baroque. Even the interior of the Cathedral is incredibly rich and sumptuous. But the most beautiful item of all, even more impressive than the splendid chapels, than the magnificent *choir-stalls* with their carved woodwork and alabaster decorations, than the *Chapter Room* with its XVI century frescoes, or the *Vestry* frescoed by Luca Giordano and where there are masterpieces by El Greco (one of these is the famous *Expolio* painted in 1577), Titian and Goya, and even more impressive than the two-storey *cloisters* created over an antique Jewish market in the XIV century to fulfil the wish of Pedro de Tenorio, the Portuguese Archbishop and benefactor of the city – is the polychromatic *Retable* that spreads out behind the High Altar, depicting scenes from the New Testament. A splendid *Nativity* dominates the centre, and higher up is an expressive *Crucifixion*.

traits painted with evident Titian influence, and the religious works of art produced for Toledo's churches. He died in 1614 while still in Toledo. Moreover, the house where he is believed to have lived is now a museum in his honour; this is in the old Jewish part of the city and still preserves some interesting features from the past.

The kitchen in El Greco's museum-house in Toledo.

However, above all, a wonderful collection of his works can be found here, including the famous, intricate *Panorama of Toledo* and the series dedicated to *Christ and the Apostles*.

The **Museo de Santa Cruz**, housed within the hospital bearing the same name and built by Cardinal Mendoza during the XVI century, contains many paintings by El Greco, among which are the *Assumption of the Virgin* (1613) and this magnificent *Annunciation* (left), extremely intense and modern due to its unusual choice of colours, and because of certain features that were constant themes in El Greco's work: faces, bodies, shapes, all lengthened to the extreme, which according to some critics were not the fruit of an intended style but were due, rather, to some disorder which had always afflicted the artist's eyesight.

One of the more profound and expressive works by El Greco is decidedly the *Entierro del Conde de Orgaz* (the *Funeral of the Count of Orgaz*, bottom), full of solemn tragedy and considered one of the best Spanish masterpieces ever painted. This 1586 work of art is in Toledo, in the beautiful old **Iglesia de Santo Tomé** (XII century) which had greatly benefited from the Count's generosity. This painting, specifically commissioned to commemorate him and made for the wall where it still hangs to this day, shows the dead Count being lifted by St. Stephen and St. Augustine to take him to Paradise. It is believed that the artist is one of the background figures, together with Miguel de Cervantes.

EL GRECO

One of the most celebrated Toledo citizens was actually an adopted citizen: known in history and the halls of fame by the significant nickname of El Greco, Domenikos Theotokopulos was in fact born in sunny Crete in 1541 and reached Toledo only in 1577, after a long period of training in Italy, under Titian in Venice, but also in Rome and in Liguria. The impact Toledo had on the artist was so intense that it changed his life: he made the city his new hometown and soon produced his principal masterpieces for Spain, like the paintings in the Escorial, commissioned by Philip II himself, or the enormous amount of por-

Toledo, capital of crafts

What was once the capital of the kingdom is still, to-day, a lively and active city that can not only boast a splendid past but can also be proud of its very prolific craftsmanship: the articles produced are exquisite and varied, ranging from weapons to ceramics, and delicious pastries and cakes.

First of all, the weapons. The Toledo swords and daggers of world fame have always been made by highly skilled craftsmen, and to this day there are still many who are capable of producing all types of metal weapons. These are all forged and engraved exclusively by hand, following techniques and procedures handed down from one generation to another. And once they are finished, the swords and daggers are given the brilliance and shine befitting all scrupulously made steel implements: this is accomplished by means of a special treatment and by paying particular attention even to the smallest detail. This specific art has evolved into the production of armours and other objects of classical damascene art. Something completely different but equally fine is the flourishing ceramic industry, which dates back to the Arabian culture that prospered in the Iberian Peninsula centuries ago; from those times on, the whole peninsula very quickly proved to be the ideal place for producing the ceramics and tiles that were used not only to decorate the interiors and exteriors of buildings, and known as *azulejos*, but also for making items for every-day use: an exquisite taste for colour, where bright hues and brilliant tones are the dominant theme, is definitely the feature common to them all.

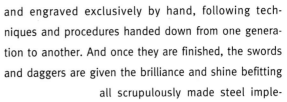

Lastly, the pastries and cakes. The typical sweet of Toledo is marzipan; a superb delicacy made of sugar and almonds unequalled elsewhere. This, too, has Arabian roots: the name actually comes from the word *mahasaban*, which the Arabs called the boxes where they stored sweetmeats and spices.

The subjects decorating the typically Iberian ceramic tiles would not be
complete without the two popular heroes created by Cervantes:
in the scene painted on the tiles in Plaza de España,
Seville, and dedicated to Ciudad Real,
Don Quixote and Sancho are depicted
starting off on their unfortunate
battles against windmills,
which are numerous
in the Castile
La Mancha
countryside.

"QVE, YO VOY A ENTRAR CON ELLOS
EN FIEL Y DESIGVAL BATALLA"

CUENCA

Since ancient times, many different cultures have recognised the great strategic value of the impregnable spur of rock, surrounded by deep, rugged gorges where the rivers Huécar and Júcar rush through, on which the town of Cuenca now stands. The Romans were the first to colonise this inaccessible place and the Arabs were the first to build a real fortress there, though all that remains now is a solitary watch tower, the *Torre de Mangana*, which stands right in the middle of the town. Cuenca laid itself open to different styles and influences throughout the centuries, thus avoiding the restrictive role of being merely a defence post. Hence, the fine **Cathedral** (XII-XVI centuries) was built, with its unmistakable Gothic façade, in which a heavier Norman influence can also be seen, however. And the Baroque XVIII century **Municipal Hall** facing

the city. Right inside one of these, in a definitely unusual but unparalleled ambience, is the *Museo de Arte Abstracto*. Then there are the famous *Casas Colgadas*, built in the XIV century, the favourite summer residences of members of the Spanish Royal Family for many years.

Left: the picturesque façade of Cuenca Cathedral, with its three large embrasured doorways. In effect, all the decorations in the large church, which took four centuries to complete, are extremely lavish and elaborate, like the detail shown above (the Defeat of Lutheran Heresy, *in the Cathedral Vestry).*
Below: one of the astonishing suspended houses; built on the edge of the rock on which Cuenca stands, these hang right over the cliffs and are the symbol of the city.

the *Plaza Mayor* was erected centuries afterwards. Then there is the interesting **Museo Arqueológico** that holds splendid, significant relics of Cuenca's thousand-odd years of history, from prehistoric times to the late XVII century. And the innovative **Museo de Arte Abstracto**, expressly conceived to exhibit items of Spanish abstract art. But, above all, the real emblems of Cuenca emerged; the **suspended houses** (or *casas colgadas*) that overhang the rocky edges of the cliffs all round the perimeter of

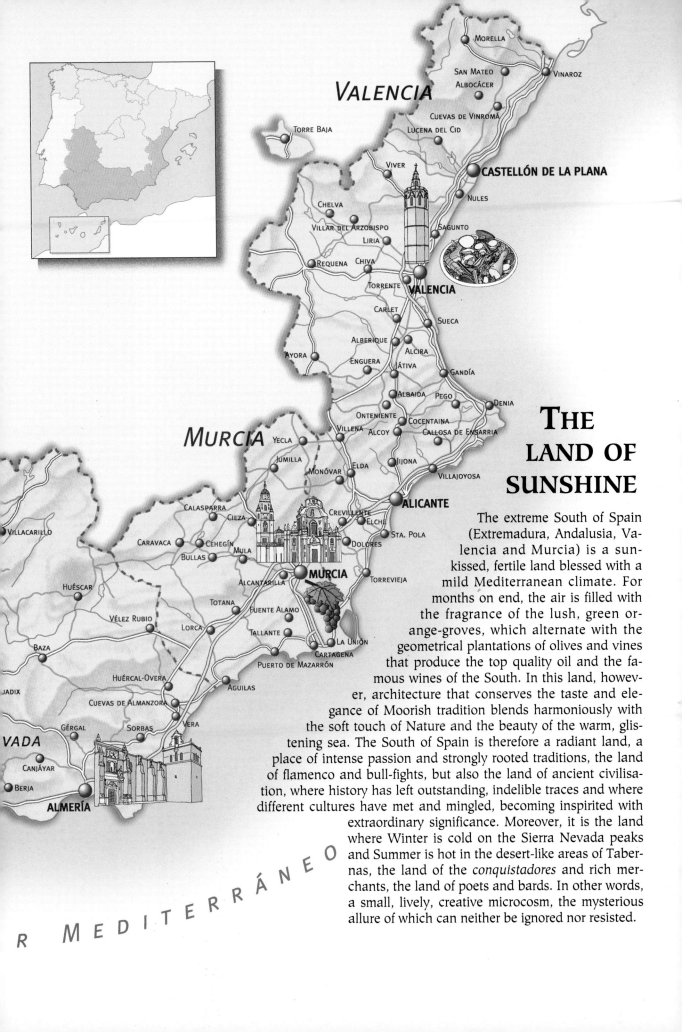

VALENCIA

MORELLA

SAN MATEO
ALBOCÁCER
VINAROZ

CUEVAS DE VINROMÁ

TORRE BAJA
LUCENA DEL CID

VIVER
CASTELLÓN DE LA PLANA

NULES

CHELVA

VILLAR DEL ARZOBISPO
LIRIA
SAGUNTO

REQUENA
CHIVA

TORRENTE
VALENCIA

CARLET
SUECA

ALBERIQUE
ALCIRA

AYORA
ENGUERA
JÁTIVA
GANDÍA

ALBAIDA
PEGO
DENIA

ONTENIENTE
COCENTAINA

MURCIA
YECLA
VILLENA
ALCOY
CALLOSA DE ENSARRIA

JUMILLA
ELDA
JIJONA

MONÓVAR
VILLAJOYOSA

ALICANTE

CALASPARRA
CIEZA
CREVILLENTE

VILLACARILLO
CARAVACA
CEHEGÍN
MULA
ELCHE
STA. POLA

BULLAS
DOLORES

ALCANTARILLA
MURCIA
TORREVIEJA

HUÉSCAR
TOTANA
FUENTE ALAMO

VÉLEZ RUBIO
TALLANTE
LA UNIÓN

LORCA
CARTAGENA

BAZA
PUERTO DE MAZARRÓN

JADIX
HUÉRCAL-OVERA
AGUILAS

CUEVAS DE ALMANZORA

GÉRGAL
SORBAS
VERA

VADA
CANJÁYAR

BERJA

ALMERÍA

R MEDITERRÁNEO

THE LAND OF SUNSHINE

The extreme South of Spain (Extremadura, Andalusia, Valencia and Murcia) is a sun-kissed, fertile land blessed with a mild Mediterranean climate. For months on end, the air is filled with the fragrance of the lush, green orange-groves, which alternate with the geometrical plantations of olives and vines that produce the top quality oil and the famous wines of the South. In this land, however, architecture that conserves the taste and elegance of Moorish tradition blends harmoniously with the soft touch of Nature and the beauty of the warm, glistening sea. The South of Spain is therefore a radiant land, a place of intense passion and strongly rooted traditions, the land of flamenco and bull-fights, but also the land of ancient civilisation, where history has left outstanding, indelible traces and where different cultures have met and mingled, becoming inspired with extraordinary significance. Moreover, it is the land where Winter is cold on the Sierra Nevada peaks and Summer is hot in the desert-like areas of Tabernas, the land of the *conquistadores* and rich merchants, the land of poets and bards. In other words, a small, lively, creative microcosm, the mysterious allure of which can neither be ignored nor resisted.

GUADALUPE

Legends narrate that, during the XIV century, a shepherd boy found a wooden statue of the Virgin Mother and Child abandoned in the woods and that this soon became worshipped by the population. The turreted, fortified **Guadalupe Monastery** was consequently built in 1340 on the spot where the image was found, while a settlement gradually grew and expanded all round it. Even the con-vent grew and increased its power, particularly as a result of royal patronage: during the XV century it already had a pharmacy, three hospitals, a library, a famous medical and grammar school and ceramic and copper works, and many skilled copyists and illuminators were at work there. The first natives brought over by Columbus from the New World were baptised here at the beginning of the XV century. And large crowds of pilgrims still come here to worship the miraculous Guadalupe Virgin.

The Virgin of Guadalupe, dressed in precious paraments: the faces of both Mary and Child are blackened by smoke from candles and votive lamps.

Above: the Roman Theatre in Mérida, where theatrical works are still performed and much appreciated. Right: a small Phoenician bronze statue covered in gold, now kept in the Archaeological Museum in Madrid.

MÉRIDA

Founded in the year 25 BC by the ambassador Publius Caritius, the small *Augusta Emerita* (now Mérida) was the capital city of the western province of Lusitania and was equipped with all the structures required for life in a Roman city: a large **Theatre**, an **Amphitheatre**, gardens, an 800 metre-long **bridge** that crosses the River Milagros, an **aqueduct** at Los Milagros, just outside the city and, naturally, **temples** (like the splendid one dedicated to the goddess Diana), **triumphal arches** and elegant houses, decorated with *mosaics* and *frescoes*. All magnificent constructions which, in spite of invasion by the Visigoths and then the Arabs, have continued to stand in fairly good condition to this day, making Mérida one of the most interesting archaeological sites in the whole of Spain.

Lost civilisations

Many great civilisations passed through Mérida, leaving traces like those seen in the local **Museo Nacional de Arte Romano** and the equally interesting **Museo de Arte Visigodo**, which both exhibit objects of great historical and artistic significance. But in Estremadura and in nearby Andalusia there are traces of yet another culture, know as 'Tartesso Culture' from the name given in ancient times to this land rich in metals. The rulers of the seas and trading, the Phoenicians, were attracted by all these riches and had tried ever since the VIII century BC to take over the entire region, but they encountered the proud resistance of the Tartessians. The conflicts continued in a succession of events until the arrival of the Carthaginians, who prevailed once and for all over the ancient Hispanic culture round only during the III century BC.

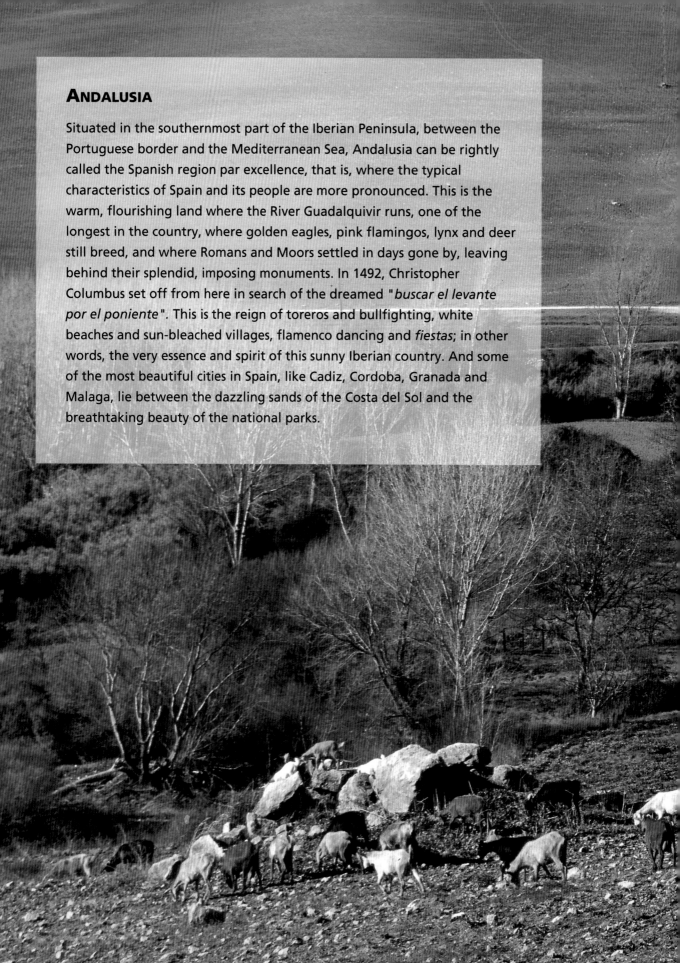

ANDALUSIA

Situated in the southernmost part of the Iberian Peninsula, between the Portuguese border and the Mediterranean Sea, Andalusia can be rightly called the Spanish region par excellence, that is, where the typical characteristics of Spain and its people are more pronounced. This is the warm, flourishing land where the River Guadalquivir runs, one of the longest in the country, where golden eagles, pink flamingos, lynx and deer still breed, and where Romans and Moors settled in days gone by, leaving behind their splendid, imposing monuments. In 1492, Christopher Columbus set off from here in search of the dreamed "*buscar el levante por el poniente*". This is the reign of toreros and bullfighting, white beaches and sun-bleached villages, flamenco dancing and *fiestas*; in other words, the very essence and spirit of this sunny Iberian country. And some of the most beautiful cities in Spain, like Cadiz, Cordoba, Granada and Malaga, lie between the dazzling sands of the Costa del Sol and the breathtaking beauty of the national parks.

El Rocio

Every year between May and June, El Rocio, a little town not far from Seville, becomes the destination of a mass pilgrimage, or *romería* as it's called, which summons pilgrims from all over the country. These present-day 'romei' travel to the town by means of all sorts of transport to pay homage to the XIII century, miraculous image of the Virgin Mother kept in the Iglesia de Nuestra Señora del Rocio, the subdued but elegant sanctuary and source of pride of this small Andalusian town. The scenes that take place during the solemn procession are quite remarkable: even before it starts, men compete for the privilege of bearing the heavy, richly adorned statue of the Madonna that has to be carried through the streets. Thereafter, throngs of pilgrims, including the members of many Brotherhoods, all make way for the sacred image to pass, then literally swarm around it in a suffocating embrace that almost submerges those carrying the canopy. An extraordinary, spectacular event, in a deeply religious atmosphere.

The Patio de los Arrayanes with the Comares Tower, a crenellated fortress 45 metres high.

Bottom: a detail of the exquisite marble and azulejos decoration in the Salón de los Embajadores.

GRANADA

Granada is an unparalleled city, protected in the North by the majestic Sierra Nevada and its high peaks, snow-capped until Spring, and facing South towards the warmest sea of all Spain, the delightful Costa del Sol. Furthermore, Granada has an abundance of water, which rushes down the mountainsides before running into the thousands of streams that make their way around palaces and courtyards, gardens and squares. This element was particularly appreciated by the Arabian dynasties that were the first to give the city its sparkling splendour. In effect, it was the Arabs who actually founded Granada, near the Roman settlement called *Illiberis*, and as the Moors became more powerful the Andalusian city rapidly expanded, to become the capital of a great kingdom in 1235 under the splendid Nasridi dynasty. Because of its advantageous position between North-African territories and the Christian states farther North, the city soon enjoyed economical prosperity and a lively cultural and artistic life. Hence, merchants and craftsmen, as well as distinguished scientists and illustrious scholars were soon seen in the palaces and streets of Granada, and its fame as a cultural centre quickly swept over the borders of the kingdom. The level of vigour and power reached by the city was such that even when the Catholic Monarchs conquered this last remaining Arabian stronghold – after eight years of fighting and two years of siege, in 1492 Ferdinand and Isabella managed to drive out the last Moorish king, Boabdil, by then weakened by domestic feuds – its cultural strength remained untarnished. Nevertheless, the typically Arabian appearance that had distinguished the city changed as the Renaissance-style set in and new elements were added: churches, convents, towers, bell-towers, palaces and hospitals. The city continued to be active and prosperous throughout the centuries that followed, except for two critical moments from 1568 to 1571: during the uprising of the *Moriscos* (the Muslims converted after the *Reconquista*), harshly repressed by King Philip II, the first step towards their expulsion that was sanctioned by Philip III in

Above, the delightful Palacio del Partal, with its luxuriant gardens and the customary stone lions (below is a detail) that keep guard in silence.
The other illustrations show the Patio de los Leones, surrounded by white marble columns and elegant decorations.
Twelve archaic, stylised lions hold up the ancient fountain in the centre of the patio.

1609; then again in the XIX century, when the city went through a transient decline, but it nevertheless recuperated by applying judicious reappraisal and redevelopment right up to the XX century. Nowadays, much of Moorish Granada still gleams bright, and the monument that is more resplendent than any other is definitely the **Alhambra**, the most striking, best preserved Arabian palace in the whole world, or the 'Vermilion Castle' as it is called because of the red clay used for its walls, standing on the top of the hill that dominates the city and with the Sierra Nevada peaks in the background. This impressive scenery was chosen by Alhamar, first sovereign of the Nasridi dynasty, for the seat of his court, and in 1238 he built the first nucleus of what was to become an immense architectural complex. His successors vied with one another to expand it, embellish it, decorate it and fortify it, to the extent that the walls protecting the summit of the hill ended up embracing a whole series of buildings, and its towers, palaces, rooms, gardens were so beautiful that even the Catholic Monarchs chose it immediately on their arrival for their resi-

dence, taking it over practically just as they found it. A series of fortified gates lead to the XIII century **Alcazaba**, a sturdy, well-fortified stronghold constructed to guard over the royal quarters, which contrast greatly against it with their delicate finishings. These royal abodes were built around two principal, exquisite courtyards: the *Patio de los Arrayanes* (or the 'Myrtle Courtyard' as it is called, because of the fragrant myrtle growing around the fountain) led off the part used by the sovereign and his court for public activities, and the *Patio de los Leones*, surrounded by 124 columns, which was outside the private chambers of the royal family. In the first part of this phantasmagoria of courtyards, fountains and gardens, one finds the spectacular

*The lavishly decorated setting of the Golden Chapel
inside the Cathedral.*

Sala del Mexuar or 'Council Chamber', substantially remodelled by Charles V and later transformed into an oratory; the *Salón de los Embajadores*, the enormous throne room built between 1334 and 1354, decorated with mosaics and stucco work and with a splendid illustration of the Muslim cosmos and its seven heavens covering the ceiling; the *Sala de la Barakha*, with its magnificent cedar wood ceiling, reconstructed after a terrible fire in 1890 had destroyed it. In the private family quarters one finds the great *Baños Reales*, and in particular the *Sala de las Dos Hermanas* (so-called because of the twin marble slabs beside the fountain) with its unmistakable beehive dome, the *Sala de los Reyes* once used for legendary banquets, the *Sala de los Abencerrajes*, from the name of a rival noble family King Boabdil had murdered here. And all around, luxurious gardens, some rooms created by Charles V and a whole **palace**, now a museum, built for the Emperor in 1526 seeing he was considering moving his capital to Granada, and above all, the **Palacio del Partal**, the oldest building in the Alhambra, a pillared pavilion topped by a wide tower. On the whole, the impression visitors get is that of being in some magic place where light, water, decorations, plants all blend in an enchanted dance: and though everything is made out of humble materials like wood, clay, stucco and ceramic, it is worked exquisitely and assembled with skill.

However, Granada is not only an Arabian city: its conquest determined the complete reunification of Spain under the Catholic Monarchs, and Ferdinand and Isabella, who were fully aware of the symbolic consequence, wanted to be buried here; this triggered a pressing desire of emula-

tion that involved noble families as well as Christian institutions, and secured the city many fine sacred monuments. The royal couple were given appropriate burials when Enrique de Egas began building the Gothic **Royal Chapel** between 1505 and 1507; but Ferdinand and Isabella are not the only ones to rest there in the crypt, since their daughter, Johanna the

Above: the colourfully painted statues representing Ferdinand of Aragona and Isabella of Castile kneeling in prayer. Below: the Pietà by Maestro de la Sangre, in the Vestry of the Royal Chapel.

One of the panoramic parapets of the Alhambra, looking towards the city and the sister hill called Albaicín.

The Bañuelo, the ancient Arabian Baths in the Albaicín district.

Mad and her husband, Philip the Handsome, have their graves there too. Their *reclining figures* carved in Carrara marble by the Florentine Domenico Fancelli lie on front of the altar, protected by a splendid *wrought-iron grating* (*reja*) by Maestro Bartolomé de Jaén (1518). In 1523, that is, two years after the solemn funeral of the Catholic Monarchs, the same Enrique de Egas started construction on the majestic **Cathedral**, building it next to the Royal Chapel; work was concluded in a more definite Renaissance style by Diego de Siloé. This great church, consecrated in 1561 but not really finished until 1703, has five spacious naves leading onto a series of chapels, all lavishly decorated (the *Main Chapel* is quite spectacular), and is illuminated by daylight shining through the XVI century stained-glass windows created by Juan del Campo on designs by Siloé himself. The West façade is the work of Alonso Cano from Granada, who is actually buried inside the Cathedral. The *Vestry* of the Royal Chapel is also worth mentioning: this is now one of the most important museums in the city and here one can find not only sacred objects, *Isabella's crown* and *Ferdinand's sword*, but also splendid paintings like work by Van der Weyden, Memling and other fine examples of Flemish art, as well as Botticelli's *Christ in the Garden of Olives*.

The panorama of the city from the top of the Al-hambra hill is breathtaking, as is the view of the sister hill, **Albaicín**, site of the first Arabian settlement at the beginning of Moorish reign. The Arabs decided to return to this hill immediately after the *Reconquista* instead of abandoning Granada, and remained there until they were expelled from Spain in 1609. Therefore, it is not just by chance that everything around here still has a Moorish flavour, from the steep, narrow streets to the white-washed houses, from the great palaces decorated with stucco work and brightened with magnificent gardens to the numerous churches (*Santa Ana, San Nicolás, San Salvador*), all built over the thirty-odd mosques that had gradually appeared around the first fortress. This characteristic, picturesque district also has well-preserved **Arabian Baths**, the oldest in the whole country, built during the XI century in a rough, unadorned style, so entirely different from those that can be seen in the Royal Chambers in the Alhambra. Yet, the light flickering through the octagonal openings in the ceiling creates a sort of star-spangled canopy and a fascinating sight. In addition, the very old Roman and Visigoth capitals placed on top of the columns to bear the arcades that project towards the vaulted ceiling are undeniably appealing.

Sufficient to make the *Bañuelo* one of the favourite spots visited by tourists when in Granada.

Gypsy Granada

The Spanish Gypsies probably came from Africa and arrived in the peninsula in mediaeval times, bringing with them a culture bearing distinct signs of the Indian origin of this people. Over the ages, their traditions, dances and melodies gradually blended with those of passionate Andalusia (an example is the influence on the flamenco), the region where many of them stayed. There is still a large group of gypsies in Grana-

Female gypsies and, on the left, the famous Cueva Zambra de la Rojo, *in the heart of the Albaicín area.*

da, where they live in the old, characteristic *cuevas* on the Albaicín, a district that besides being Arabian is decidedly Gypsy.

133

THE GRANADA CHARTERHOUSE

In 1516, a noble and Christian knight called Fernando González de Córdoba, better known as 'El Gran Capitán', founded an impressive Charterhouse just out of Granada, for monks devoted to St. Bruno; only the Church, Vestry, Cloisters and some annexes remain standing but are sufficient for giving an idea of the magnificence of this structure, so austere and unadorned on the outside. Besides the fine *paintings* hanging on the walls of the nave, one of which is by Sánchez Cotán who was actually a monk in the Charterhouse, underneath the *dome* of the church (frescoed by Antonio Palomino) a phantasmagorical *canopy* supported by spiral pillars stands over the main altar and the tabernacle: a lively *churrigueresque* medley that recalls the adjacent *Vestry*, produced by Luis de Arévalo and Luis Cabello with an incredible abundance of decoration. The *Cloisters* are much more subdued, like the adjacent Gothic-style *Refectory* where another beautiful piece by Sánchez Cotán can be admired, *Scenes in the Life of St. Bruno.*

Extraordinarily decorative phantasmagoria enhances the churrigueresque-*style Vestry of the Charterhouse.*

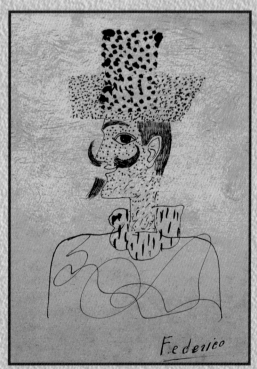

Salvador Dalí, Self-portrait dedicated to Lorca, *ink on paper, 22 x 16 cm, Mollet (Barcelona), Juan Abello Prat collection.*

Federico García Lorca

Federico García Lorca, son of a landowner and destined to become not only a sensitive, creative poet, but also an expert on Andalusian spirit, was born in Fuentevaqueros (Granada) in 1898. His knowledge of Andalusian temperament was no doubt due to his infancy in the countryside of this region, his studies at Almería and in the faculty of Letters and Law at Granada University. Yet, Castile was the place that influenced his first work, *Impressions and Landscapes* (1918). Moreover, Madrid attracted him towards music, the theatre and art, and gave him the opportunity to meet great artists like Dalí and Buñuel. But it was Andalusian spirit that was behind the work that brought him success and exerted so much influence on modern literature, from *Songs* (1927) to *Mariana Pineda* (still in 1927), from *Gypsy Ballads* (1928) to *Poema del Canto Jondo* (1931), from *Blood Wedding* (1933) to *Yerma* (1934) and *The House of Bernarda Alba* (1936). And he met with his tragic destiny in Andalusia: having gone back to Granada as he always did every Summer, the poet was arrested in July 1936 by the Francoist Civil Guards and, although he had never participated directly in any political activity, he was shot on 19th August of that year.

The majestic, immense Gothic Cathedral in Seville, built on a cross layout. The Giralda soars high above it, the ancient minaret transformed into a bell-tower with elaborate balconies and belfries (below) crowned by the Triumph of Faith, *the bronze weathervane (giraldillo) which gives it its name.*

SEVILLE

According to tradition, Seville was founded by Hercules who appears to have played a very active role in the many ancient legends concerning the origins of Andalusia. Prose-like verses narrate of a prosperous Phoenician settlement occupied first by the Greeks and then by the Carthaginians, followed by the Romans. In effect, Seville simply followed the same fate as most of the large cities in this region: after being conquered by the Visigoths who made it the capital of their kingdom, it was conquered by the Arabs in 712 and flourished and grew under their dominion until it could rival the nearby Cordoba in size and splendour. During the XIII century, King Ferdinand III triumphantly took over, and was ultimately buried here, leaving his emblems forever in the city. In the XV century, the Catholic Monarchs established their court here in the old Moorish buildings. However, it was the Discovery of America and the consequent, expanding whirlwind of trade and commerce that brought Seville to the height of its glory, and to a considerable increase in population. The dreadful plague epidemic in 1649, however, was the start of a slow but progressive decline from which the city has never fully recovered, even though it still preserves traces of its past glory and maintains its unquestionably lively culture, besides continuing in its role as administrative capital of the region, headquarters of the autonomous government and focal point of its social and political upset.

One of the most famous and significant monuments in the city is certainly the striking **Cathedral**, built on the spot where the main mosque used to stand and of which two impressive remains can still be seen: the fertile *Patio de los Naranjos* (the Orange-tree Courtyard, where worshippers performed their ritual cleansing and which, through the *Puerta del Perdón*, still leads to the sacred building) and the imposing, almost 100 metres high *minaret* built in the XII century and later skilfully modified to become the bell-tower of the new Cathedral. On the top of it stands the characteristic bronze weather-

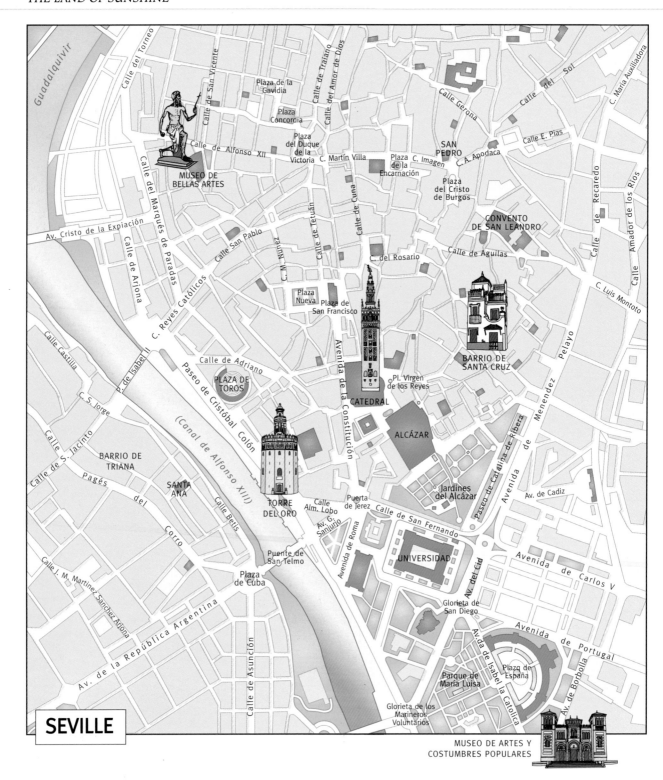

SEVILLE

MUSEO DE ARTES Y
COSTUMBRES POPULARES

vane representing the *Triumph of Faith*: this was erected in 1568 in place of the four golden globes that had been destroyed previously in an earthquake, and the tower that is now a symbol of the city is familiarly called the *Giralda*, from the Spanish for weather-vane, *Giraldillo*. The Cathedral itself was started in Gothic style in 1402, but became more and more Renaissance as the years passed. A series of the best architects and artists of the moment were commissioned to build what was to be-come one of the biggest basilicas in the whole of Christendom, with its 40 columns illuminated by sunlight shining through 93 stained-glass windows: Juan Normán, Pedro de Toledo, Gil de Hontañón (who built the *dome*), Murillo, Zurbarán, Alonso Cano, to mention only a few. Then there were the sculptors (like Andrea della Robbia and Miguel Perrin), the engravers and chisellers (from Nufro Sánchez who was responsible for the exquisite woodwork in the *choir-stalls*, to Francisco de Salamanca who forged the beautiful items in wrought iron). An entire army of skilled workers and artists were therefore assigned the task of building this majestic, gigantic work of art with beautiful chapels opening onto five splendid naves. And even the spectacular, phantasmagorical Gothic *Retable* which dominates the *High Altar* has few rivals regards size: 200 square metres of skilful carving and over a thousand figures relating important episodes in the *Lives of the Virgin Mary and Christ*. Though it was started by Danckaert the Flemish artist in 1482, other artists worked on it and did not finish it until 1521, and the elements on the sides are the work of Diego Vázquez, Nufro de Ortega and Juan López, among others, between 1550 and 1564. The adjacent *Royal Chapel*, started by Martín de Gainza in 1551 and finished by Juan de Maeda in 1575, is probably less striking with its more sober Renaissance style, but it is certainly just as beautiful. Alphonse the Wise and his mother, who first inspired his dreams of conquest, are buried in this chapel. The incorrupt body of the saintly King Ferdinand III lies in a lavish sarcophagus on front of the main altar. But two other magnificent elements in the Cathedral that deserve mention are the XVI century Vestries: the *Main Vestry* which, besides holding the *Treasure* of the Basilica, also contains a silver *tabernacle* by Juan de Arfe and the *Tablas Alfonsínas*, precious

Above: a splendid detail of the gigantic Gothic Retable that embellishes the Main Chapel of the Cathedral. The Nativity can be seen in the centre of the scene, with the Virgin Mary represented above it. There are also many Saints from Seville portrayed in the Retable, as well as Santa María de la Sede, Patron Saint of the Cathedral and the city. Left: the impressive tomb of Christopher Columbus with the sovereigns of Aragona, Castile, León and Navarra solemnly bearing the navigator's coffin.

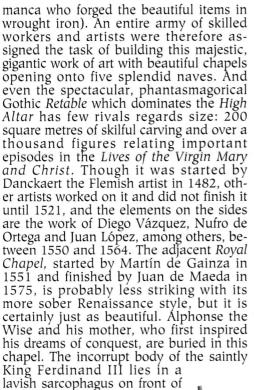

astronomical tables forming a triptych, donated by Alphonse X; and the lovely *Chalice Vestry*, a real museum where *paintings* by Goya (depicting the two Sevillian Saints, Justa and Rufina), Murillo, Morales and Tristán can be seen. Then, a monument that attracts a lot of attention and curiosity is the spectacular *Tomb of Christopher Columbus*, one of the last, original additions to the Cathedral, lying at the head of the transept: made by Arturo Mélida in the XIX century and brought here from Havana Cathedral in 1899, the tomb is composed of a magnificent sculptural group in which four solemnly adorned figures representing the four kingdoms of Spain (Aragona, Castile, León and Navarra) are the pall-bearers of the famous explorer's coffin.

HOLY WEEK

Religion and folklore blend together in Andalusia for Holy Week, seven days of solemn celebrations throughout the whole of Spain, with throngs

participating in processions and following parades with enormous floats practically everywhere. Nevertheless, Andalusia is the place where participation is most devote and enthusiastic during the week between

Palm Sunday and Easter Day. In Seville, for example, about a hundred huge, golden floats called *pasos*, loaded with crucifixes and votive images that

sometimes recreate episodes of the Passion, are taken up and down the streets many times. On Holy Wednesday, a tremendous detonation like a clap of thunder is fired to shatter the silence in the Cathedral, recalling the time when the veil in the Jerusalem Temple was ripped. Another identical 'clap of thunder' is produced during Midnight Mass on the night between Holy Saturday and Easter Sunday, and is the signal for all bells to start ringing. The huge crowds always participate actively in these celebrations, reciting prayers and singing hymns, some of which

are very old and known as *saetas*. At the same time, repentant sinners covered from head to toe in long tunics and pointed hoods, walk the streets non-stop and plead forgiveness for their sins.

Views of the Parque de María Luisa: above, the famous Plaza de España; centre left, the Museo Arqueológico and, below, the Plaza de América, with the pavilion that holds the Folk Art and Costume Museum in the background.

On the previous pages, two views of the striking Salón de los Embajadores.

However, Seville is not just the city with the *Giralda*: an Arabian heart still throbs in the beautiful **Reales Alcázares**, once surrounded by long walls and composed of many buildings until it gradually dwindled because of fires, earthquakes and particularly reconstruction and modifications. Hence, only the walls have survived, with the *Puerta del León* and the *Torre del Oro* (built in 1220 as a watch tower, along with its sister tower on the opposite embankment of the River Guadalquivir; the two towers were connected over the river by means of a sturdy chain meant to stop enemy ships passing through), and the *Patio del Yeso* (the Chalk Courtyard). The original buildings were substituted with a magnificent *palace* designed in *Mudéjar* style for Peter I of Castile by Muslim architects from Granada and Toledo and finished in the XIV century; thereafter it was extended several times, first for Charles V (who had sumptuous chambers added on) then for Philip IV. The great *Alcázar*, surrounded by lush gardens, is built around two exquisite and luxurious courtyards: the *Patio de las Doncellas* (the Young Maidens' Courtyard) with XVI century ceramic decorations and Arabian-style carving, which leads off from the rooms reserved for public ceremonies – one of these is the *Hall with the Charles V Ceiling*, called thus because of the Renaissance carvings in cedar-wood, and another is the spectacular *Salón de los Embajadores* which dates back to Peter I, except for the dome which was added on in 1427 –; and the *Patio de las Muñecas* (the Dolls' Courtyard) where everyday, family life went on. In the *Admirals' Halls* inside the *Alcázares* there is also the *Casa de la Contratación*, designed for Queen Isabella, where

some of the most important voyages towards the New World were planned, including Magellan's circumnavigation of the globe which started from here.

Other splendours can be seen elsewhere in the relatively more modern parts of Seville. Like the **Parque de María Luisa**, for example, the romantic park made for this princess in 1893 and skilfully landscaped by Jean Forestier, the Director of the Bois de Boulogne, to accommodate the 1929 Iberian-American Exhibition. The memory of that event still lives on in some of the creations, like the **Plaza de España**, built with traditional materials (red bricks, enamelled tiles, and with colours and fantasy galore) and its famous *benches* where ceramic-tile panels reproduce allegories of the 53 Spanish provinces; or the **Plaza de América**, animated by fountains and pigeons and enlivened by terraces and gardens. Nearby, one of the Exhibition pavilions (the *Pabellón Mudéjar*) now houses an interesting **Folk Art and Costume Museum** (*Museo*

de Artes y Costumbres Populares*), which is an amusing detailed illustration of everyday life in Seville: furniture, utensils, clothing, ceramics, jewellery, but also tradition, devotion, pastimes, games, bulls and toreros. Another pavilion, the *Pabellón de las Bellas Artes*, holds the city's **Archaeological Museum**, one of the most important in Spain as far as ancient Roman relics and sculptures are concerned, as well as items traceable to the native Tartesso civilisation. Many of the Roman pieces exhibited come from excavations in the nearby *Itálica*, one of the first Roman cities in Spain, founded by Scipio Africanus in 206 BC.

Left: a fine example of Roman statuary, discovered in the Itálica excavations. Below: the austere Torre del Oro, which probably owes its name to the golden azulejos that distinguished it in the past. The turret was added on only in the XVIII century.

THE EXPO

The year 1992 was a very important one for Spain since it became the centre of international interest due to a series of events occurring simultaneously: that was the five hundredth anniversary of the discovery of America, an event that changed world history and in which the great Iberian Peninsula had played a fundamental role. Hence, Barcelona was selected to hold the 1992 *Olympic Games*, in spectacular and futuristic scenery, whereas Seville was chosen as the site for the *Expo '92*, an extremely important world-wide event, which partially changed the appearance of this peaceful Andalusian city. The most appropriate site for the Universal Exhibition, where all the most recent technological and scientific discoveries would be presented, was identified in the *Isla de la Cartuja*, on the banks of the River Guadalquivir. This was where parks were created with educational and cultural themes and where futuristic structures and innovative pavilions, worthy of such an event that looked to the future, were built to house the over 100 participating nations. A monorail railway with an ultra modern train took visitors from one section to another, from the metallic *Castile and León Pavilion* to the unmistakable steeply leaning, blue tower which held the *Andalusia Pavilion*. Not even the XIV century *Santa María de las Cuevas* charterhouse, famous for having accommodated Christopher Columbus among others, 'escaped' from all this; on the contrary, once it had been appropriately restructured it was called upon to participate directly in the event. And when it was all over, these ambitious, striking monuments to the optimism of Mankind in the future, nearly all remained and continue to dominate this enormous part of the city which, due to the exciting and educational experience it had gone through, had definitely changed. Like the *Navigator's Pavilion,* for example, an authentic naval museum on the river embankment, or the *Lago de España* that is now the focal point of a large fairground opened in 1997 and renamed *Isla Mágica*. The exploits of the navigators and explorers of the New World who started their journeys from Seville during the XVI century are all re-enacted here with spectacular pride.

The Patio de los Naranjos, where five fountains gush amongst the orange trees, looks out to the Mosque-Cathedral.
Right: the lavishly decorated interior of the dome of the Cathedral.

CORDOBA

The magnificence of Arabian civilisation reached one of its highest peaks in Cordoba, for centuries the capital of a caliphate that had influence even farther North than tiny Andalusia. History tells of it being a Carthaginian city conquered by the Romans, who made it the capital of Ulterior Spain. Seneca the Elder, Seneca the Younger and Lucan were all born here, and the Goths arrived in 572, followed by the Arabs in 711. With the arrival of the Arabs, Cordoba's history changed: all the emirs had a predilection for this city, which was the most intensely populated and modern city in the western world during the X century, with its 300 mosques, splendid palaces, public baths, an efficient sewerage system, innovative public lighting and the cultural contribution of distinguished scholars, from Maimonides, the Jewish philosopher and physician, to Averroé. Then, in the XI century, the emirate split up and Cordoba began to slowly decline: conquered by Ferdinand III the Saint in 1236, it experienced the tormented life of a frontier city until the unification of Spain under the Christian flag and lived in a sort of limbo as far as the XX century,

ever enthusiastically rediscovering its treasures. However, Cordoba has remained principally an Arabian city, as can be seen in its most famous, unique monument: the **Mosque-Cathedral**. Between 785 and 787, Abd al Rahman had a first mosque built, with eleven naves standing perpendicular to the *Patio de los Naranjos*, where worshippers performed their ritual ablutions amongst the orange trees. Abd al Rahman II extended the naves towards the River Guadalquivir, which is crossed

here by the great *Puente Romano*. Then Al Hakam II built the elegant *Mihrab*, where a copy of the Koran was kept on the bottom wall until Al-Mansur extended the prayer room and added a further eight naves. This resulted in a forest of more than 800 marble, granite and jasper *columns* bearing the typical red and white striped arches. And in 1523, Charles V had a Catholic Cathedral grafted into this stone forest but it was not finished until 250 years later, which meant that it was influenced by many

Three marble figures representing Ferdinand and Isabella welcoming Christopher Columbus stand in the gardens of the Alcázar de los Reyes Cristianos.

the lavish Baroque *dome* of the church and the rich *chapels*, one of which is the *Capilla de Villaviciosa* that was erected even before the Cathedral, having been built in *Mudéjar* style inside the mosque in 1371. All the same, in this substantially Arabian city that also has an ancient Jewish district, another strong trace of the powerful Catholic Monarchs is seen in the elegant **Alcázar de los Reyes Cristianos**, a residential complex ordered by Alphonse XI during the XIV century. This palace, which was once the seat of the king and his court, has now been transformed into a *museum* where Roman sarcophagi and mosaics can be admired. Nevertheless, the magnificent *gardens*, pervaded with Arabian-like harmony, protected by crenellated walls and towers, and embellished with terraces and streams, still maintain their ancient allure with their silent, enchanted atmosphere.

Left: a view of the amazing forest of columns inside the Mosque-Cathedral.

Below: another splendid view of the Alcázar gardens, filled with fountains and lush, green vegetation.

styles, from Gothic to Baroque. Even the minaret was recycled and inserted into the *Alminar Tower*, standing menacingly 93 metres high over the *Puerta del Perdón* (1377) that opens on to the great *patio*. Therefore, in what was once the second greatest mosque in Islam, second only to the one in the Mecca, the elegance of Arabian art lives hand in hand with

PARQUE NACIONAL COTO DOÑANA

The *Parque Nacional Coto Doñana*, source of pride to Andalusia, lies in the Southwest corner of Spain; the beauty of this nature park is outstanding, not only because of the various swamps and woods found here and there, but also for its setting along the coast, where candid dunes shift in the winds. Along the course of River Guadalquivir and as far as its estuary, deer and wild boars, shy lynxes and elegant fallow deer, rare golden eagles and delightful pink flamingos all have their habitat here, where the umbrella pines tower over thick carpets of shrubs. And during Winter, thousands of migrating birds find a sheltered haven in the almost 100,000 hectares of the park, attracted by the pleasant waters of the enormous swamps. Many years ago, the entire area was a popular game reserve (*coto*) belonging to a noble family. Then, in 1969, the whole territory was placed under naturalistic restrictions and was officially declared protected.
Since then, flora and fauna have been able to reproduce unhindered, not at all disturbed by the occasional presence of humans: visits around the park are exclusively by appointment and only a few people at a time are allowed entrance.

ALMERÍA

White-washed sunny Almería, one of the most picturesque spots in the whole of Spain, boasts one of the most imposing Moorish fortresses in the country, the **Alcazaba**, a splendid reminder of the times when this thriving trading port was one of the principal centres of the Cordoba Caliphate.

After suffering many sieges, the forbidding stronghold was finally conquered by the Christians in 1489. Following this, they added on the so-called *Torre del Homenaje*, the stout square keep in the centre, and even built a chapel in the Moorish structure. The typical district where fishermen and gypsies live, known as **La Chanca**, stretches out at the foot of the fortress. Here one can see the numerous, typical dwellings made right inside caves – the outsides of which are all gaily painted with a touch of light-hearted coquetry – or hewed out of the tuff. On the whole, it can be said that Almería has always had the advantage of favourable surroundings, and not only from a landscape point of view: the first distinct settlements in this area, around 3,000 BC, were not there just by chance. However, the beautiful sea that has been one of the town's prime sources of wealth for so many centuries, was also a potential menace for a long time in the past, since the coast suffered devastating attacks from pirates and corsairs. And it is not surprising, either, that

Above: an impressive view of the majestic Alcazaba; below, the well-appointed Almería Cathedral; on the opposite page, colourful examples of the typical dwellings made inside caves or dug out of the tuff in the picturesque La Chanca district, inhabited by fishermen and gypsies.

the **Cathedral**, which was built over an ancient mosque and reconstructed by Diego de Siloé in 1524 after a terrible earthquake, looks more like a menacing, fortified stronghold on the outside, protected as it is by towers, than a church. Inside, however, the *choir-stalls* skilfully worked by Juan de Orea give the whole building a touch of exquisite elegance.

THE FLAMENCO

One of the most spectacular, passionate elements of the colourful and fiery Andalusian nature is undoubtedly the flamenco, that rhythmic, noble dance that personifies life, with its overwhelming joys and its intense anguish. Typical of Andalusia and with a gypsy background, the flamenco as we know it today began to take shape and become more explicit only in the XVIII century, with a skilful blend of miscellaneous influences, from Moorish to Jewish, and a touch of oriental flavour. The rhythm itself, which is produced by hand-clapping, by the percussive sound of guitar chords and very often by castanets, is extremely fast, but still cannot be considered definitely classified: the dancers (the *bailaora* – the female dancer and the real leader in the performance, with her typical, brightly coloured costume that swirls out like a fan – and the *bailaor*) end up by improvising the choreography of their dance. They also glean inspiration from the warm, throaty voice of the solo singer, the *cantaor*, who accompanies the dance by singing the traditional airs now known as *cante jondo* – 'deep ballads'. In spite of the flamenco being typical of Andalusia, and although it is impregnated with deep, nostalgic melancholy while the movements are charged with vitality, it has become very popular not only in all the other Spanish regions but even farther afield, distinguishing itself throughout the world as an enthralling, captivating performance.

Above: a splendid view of Malaga Port, with the green Paseo del Parque.
Left: a side of the Cathedral, with its doorway sheltered between two typical semi-circular buttresses.

MALAGA

Sunny Malaga as we see it today is a classical, lively Andalusian city, but its complex history relates of a thousand years of significant events and great splendour. When the Phoenicians landed on the coasts of the Tartessian kingdom around 1100 BC, attracted by the considerable mining resources, in order to secure themselves a network of indispensable mainstay posts they started founding a series of colonies, the majority of which prospered very quickly. One of these colonies was *Malaca*, which very soon became a very dynamic port. Its prosperity and trading did not dwindle at all, even during the following centuries when the Greeks substituted the Phoenicians, then the Romans the Greeks, followed by the

Above: the sober gardens which soften the rough, powerful lines of the Alcazaba. Below: one of the decorations in the city park, a characteristic mosaic made with the typical azulejos.

Moors during the Christian era. It was the Moors, in fact, who built the magnificent **Alcazaba** between the VIII and XI centuries on the site of a fortified Roman settlement, right beside the imposing Theatre. This Alcazaba was a series of concentric, fortified walls intervalled with massive keeps, the highest and greatest of which was the *Torre del Homenaje,* the hub of the defence system, built during the second half of the VIII century by the same Abd al Rahman who was the founder of the Cordoba Caliphate. Spectacular fortified gateways led inside the walls and to the governor's luxurious *palace,* built in the XI century and so lavishly appointed that it could rival any of the principal Arabian palaces: elegantly decorated, it consisted in spacious courtyards, luxuriant gardens, pools and, of course, the baths so dear to Moorish culture. When this great fortress was built, Malaga was already one of the main ports in the whole area under Arabian dominion, and the city maintained this prominent position even when the Christians returned at the end of the XV century. In fact, farsighted Ferdinand and Isabella, who reconquered Malaga in 1487, did

not banish the Moors; they continued to live here and contribute to the city's prosperity right up to the beginning of the XVII century, when Philip III officially expelled them. However, as time went by the lustre of the city gradually dimmed, overshadowed by nearby Cadiz, at least until the XIX century when the ancient Phoenician colony rediscovered what had already been a great source of wealth in the past, the famous *Malaga* wine, which very quickly conquered the Eu-

ropean market. Today, the city is particularly admired as the pleasant capital of the Costa del Sol, surrounded as it is by warm seas and a profusion of modern facilities for tourism. A lot of its old, characteristic districts were seriously damaged beyond repair during the violent fighting between Liberals and Absolutists in the XIX century, when Malaga was often the centre of the events. But those who wish to visit it will nevertheless come upon some pleasant surprises: the **Cathedral**, for instance, with its curious array of styles, which was started by Diego de Siloé in 1528 but interrupted in 1783, when the second tower of the façade was still unfinished and fated to remain so; or the remains of the Roman Theatre, built during the Augustus period and abandoned in the III century – some of the relics from these excavations are displayed in the local **Museo Arqueológico**, together with remnants of Phoenician and Arabian culture –; or even the XIV century **Gibralfaro Moorish Castle** of ancient

Left: an aerial view of the Plaza de Toros in Malaga. Below: the well groomed gardens in front of the Ayuntamiento, the elegant Municipal Hall.

*Above: the sturdy walls of the Moorish Gibralfaro Castle, creating
a severe-looking background to a delightful fountain.
Below: one of the antique mosaics displayed in the archaeological
section of the Fine Arts Museum.*

Phoenician origin and reconstructed many times,
sitting high up behind the city and nowadays just a
impressive ruin, though still connected to the *Alcazaba* by a portion of the city walls. However, in this
city where Pablo Picasso was born and where the
Foundation bearing the famous artist's name is accommodated in the house where he lived as an infant, yet another of the places which deserve mention is the rich **Museo de Bellas Artes** in the XVI
century *Palacio de los Condes de Buena Vista*, a
spectacular Renaissance building standing around
two courtyards. Here there are numerous,
outstanding paintings by XVI and XVII
century Flemish artists, masterpieces
by Luis de Morales, Murillo, Ribera and, in the section dedicated
to XIX and XX artists originally
from Malaga, some of Pablo Picasso's earliest work (engravings
and etchings).
However, this attractive city on the
sea, rich in churches and folk traditions, where both Carnival and Holy
Week are celebrated with great enthusiasm, is also a city full of greenery. There
is the great 30,000 m² **Parque de Malaga,** for instance, right in the middle of the
city, where numerous species of splendid
tropical plants grow. Then, stretched out on

the hilly land behind the inhabited area, there is the
Parque Natural de los Montes de Malaga full of
a delightful network of pathways. Here in this beautiful and practically uncontaminated park, many
species of local wild-life can be seen, like wild
boars, eagles and deer, who all live free
and wild as they peacefully roam
through the beautiful
lavender fields.

BAEZA
JAÉN
ÚBEDA

The picturesque Andalusian countryside is scattered here and there with pleasant towns that contain real architectural treasures: two of these towns are Baeza and Úbeda, splendid examples of Spanish Renaissance near the *Sierra de Cazorla* – a magnificent nature park –, incredibly rich in history and majestic monuments, like the ancient *churches* in Úbeda and the great *palaces* in Baeza. But this can also be said of Jaén, near the border between Andalusia and Castile, once a compulsory stop for caravans and now a town with spectacular buildings (the most beautiful is the XVI century **Cathedral**) watched over by the menacing **Castillo de Santa Catalina**, a fortress erected by Ferdinand III in 1246 over the spot of a previous Moorish stronghold.

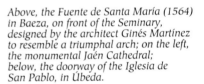

Above, the Fuente de Santa María (1564) in Baeza, on front of the Seminary, designed by the architect Ginés Martínez to resemble a triumphal arch; on the left, the monumental Jaén Cathedral; below, the doorway of the Iglesia de San Pablo, in Úbeda.

Ronda, with the stunning Puente Nuevo, dominates the valley from its rocky spur. Right: the Philip V Arch. On the following pages: the Plaza de Toros and one of the paintings Goya dedicated to bull-fighting.

RONDA

Perched high on a rock and surrounded by cliffs, divided into two parts by a 90 metre deep gorge bridged by the monumental, XIX century **Puente Nuevo**, the white-washed town of Ronda that was impregnable for many centuries and was not returned to Christendom until 1485, is an interesting place because of the remains of a Roman Theatre, its white Moorish houses, Arabian baths, splendid palaces, an elegant *Town Hall* and, above all, its grand **Plaza de Toros**, one of the oldest in Spain (1785) and the birthplace of modern bull-fighting. In fact, this was the realm of the legendary torero called Pedro Romero, who was responsible for the 'Ronda' style still in use. In September every year, one of the most popular events in the whole country is held here. The town has an interesting **Bull Museum** dedicated to the art of bull fighting and where there are even prints by Goya representing scenes in the bullring.

*"The bull is the greatest poetical
and spiritual treasure belonging to Spain"*
Federico García Lorca

THE BULL-FIGHT

Bull-fighting, which descends from ancient tauromachy, was a pastime for aristocrats for a long time until the XVIII century, when the Bourbons and legendary toreros like Pedro Romero and Pepe-Hillo transformed it into an incredibly popular and spectacular performance. Nowadays, every Spanish city, whether large or small, has its own bullring (*plaza de toros*), and the relative programme of bullfights is often linked with the festivities for their Patron Saints. Hence, at five o'clock in the afternoon, three toreros (*matadores*) enter the bullring, each with two *picadores* (toreros on horseback) and three *banderilleros* at his side, and each with two bulls to fight. Before a crowd of exited, eager spectators, this age-old challenge is repeated and braved with solemn ritual and with the enthusiasm of a work of art. The *matador* performs a series of traditional passes with his cape to joust the bull, and then he 'hands it over' to the *picadores* whose task is to tire it. Next come the *banderilleros*, who tackle the bull and stab it with their *banderillas* decorated with ribbons. However, it is the *matador* who comes back into the scene to kill the bull: armed with his sword and *muleta*, the famous red cape, he fells it with a single, well-aimed thrust. When the performance has been particularly enthralling, the spectators roar their enthusiasm and the *matador* is awarded the bull's ear as a trophy.

COSTA DEL SOL

The beautiful, sun-blessed Costa del Sol, the ancient land of Andalusian fishermen now an authentic paradise for Spanish and international tourism, stretches out where bright blue skies blend into the turquoise, crystal-clear sea, between Granada and the Strait of Gibraltar. All along the continuous strip of white sands that winds its way through the creeks and inlets of southern Andalusia, a picturesque succession of attractive seaside resorts has developed in the shade of the orange-groves: **Motril**, modern and lively; delightful **Almuñécar**; **Nerja**, famous for the enchanted atmosphere of its caves full of stalactites and stalagmites; **Torremolinos**, which developed rapidly out of an old fishing village, chaotic, full of long avenues, hotels, entertainment and particularly popular facilities for tourists; then there is quieter **Fuengirola**; and **Marbella**, a city with an age-old centre, capital of fashionable, aristocratic, luxury tourism, sufficiently sumptuous to be the spot preferred by millionaires and film stars; or **Estepona**, quiet and on a human scale; **Sotogrande**, more exclusive and elite.

All the tourists who come here, whether wealthy or not, can rest assured that no matter which resort they have chosen, the sea will always be splendid and inviting, the sky will always be clear, the facilities will be modern and top quality, and the beaches will be spacious and well-equipped. Not to mention the typical little harbours where numerous sports craft berth; or the characteristic restaurants where delicious seafood is served accompanied by the unmistakable wines of the South; the fashionable places that make night-life lively and irresistible; and the 30 or more lush-green, golf courses, for a sport that is becoming more and more popular here. And, for those who want a little bit more than just sunshine and a host of water sports, what could be better than a relaxing trip inland, to see some of the most beautiful places in Andalusia, the typical white-washed villages that stand out on the slopes of the Sierra and that have won the hearts of poets and artists through the ages, from **Mijas** to **Casares**, and **Gaucín**.

*Typical scenery along the Costa del Sol: sea and beaches galore,
numerous hotels, many ports and, as if that were not enough,
splendid golf courses.*

The elegant Cadiz Cathedral, with its unmistakable golden dome, looks imposing even from the seafront.
An elegant tower in the same style stands at each side of the Neo-classic façade.

CADIZ

Cadiz is a city surrounded by water, perched on a narrow isthmus that stretches out into the sea. The prosperous Phoenician *Gadir*, which as far back as the XII century BC traded with Tyre and Sidon, exporting eastwards the sought-after tin required to make bronze and silver (as mentioned in the Bible), the *Gades* that was a lively Roman port after the Carthaginian period and before the Moorish conquest in 711, the *Cádiz* that King Alphonse X brought back under Christendom in 1262, is still to this day an important international harbour, just as it was, in effect, immediately after the discovery of America. However, that was when its importance attracted attack by the English (Sir Francis Drake even managed to ransack it in 1587); but it was later on, during the XIX century, in this city that was temporarily capital of Spain, in the place where the Spanish Liberalists assembled in Parliament in 1812 to proclaim the first Constitution, that the ancient monuments were shattered by the tragic events of war. Nevertheless, some small but interesting churches still stand, like the XVIII century **Oratorio de San Felipe Neri**, where the Parliament held that famous meeting in 1812, and then there is the massive **Cathedral** (XVIII-XIX century), built over an older one, where Baroque and Neo-classic mingle well under the shadow of a golden *dome* – erected between 1812 and 1838 – and where magnificent paintings, as well as the splendidly carved *choirstalls* by Pedro Duque Cornejo, adorn its interior.

However, many of the vestiges of the ancient grandeur now grace the famous, well-appointed **Museo de Cádiz** laid out on three floors: the ground floor holds an interesting *Archaeological Museum* full of ancient relics discovered in the area; the first floor has a *Museum of Fine Arts* displaying paintings by Rubens, Van Eyck, Murillo, Alonso Cano, Ribera and, above all, a considerable amount of paintings by Zurbarán; the top floor is dedicated to an unusual and admirable collection of the typical Andalusian *puppets*.

The solemn Colegiata, source of pride of Jerez architecture and, below, a modern azulejo with a religious theme.

JEREZ DE LA FRONTERA

Jerez de la Frontera, a city brimming with attractions and allure, can be considered an astounding synthesis of the spirit of Andalusia: home of the famous wine, *Sherry* (*Jerez*), in its many varieties and many degrees of body and sweetness, created in the immense, much visited cellars by means of the typical *solera* technique; home of one of the most famous Spanish flamenco dancing schools; land of elegant, proud horses, the *Cartujanos*, 'Carthusians', so-called because they were kept for a long time in the fine **Charterhouse** with a Gothic court-yard just a few kilometres outside the city, and where a horse-fair was held for many years; proud of its **Real Escuela Andaluza de Arte Ecuestre**, a high class riding school. Jerez above all can boast of a magnificent historical and artistic past.

Proof of this is the majestic, elaborate **Colegiata**, a stunning background for the traditional folk festivities held throughout September to celebrate the wine-harvest; the noble remains of the XI century **Alcázar**, only partially reconstructed and with a *mosque* inside that became a church; then there are the Arabian baths, and towers, convents, palaces, plus the very un-usual and unique **Museo de Relojes**, an extraordinary collection of watches and clocks of all ages.

BEHIND SHERRY

The procedure employed to produce an excellent *Sherry* entails many steps that have been handed down throughout the centuries and which are followed almost like a solemn ritual. The Jerez wine is made from *Palomino* and *Pedro Ximénez* grapes proportionately mixed according to the desired strength. The grapes are harvested during the first half of September: the *Palomino* grapes are submitted immediately to pressing, while long straw mats await the *Pedro Ximénez* ones that have to dry out in the sun so that the sugar-content can reach its highest concentration. Pressing is carried out in cylindrical tanks, generally during the night when it is cooler. The liquid then flows out into the fermentation tanks. The next step foresees filling the casks, placed one on top of another in a pyramid: the ones highest up, the younger ones, are for the new wine, which will then be blended with the older wine contained in the casks further down the pyramid.

This system, known as *solera*, guarantees constant quality. The degree of alcohol (between 15° and 18°) is adjusted by adding wine spirit. The last step con-

sists in bottling the wine, which is drawn exclusively from the bottom casks containing the oldest wine: then the *Sherry* is ready to set out and conquer the world.

On the following pages: the flow of the tranquil Guadalete creates wide bends in the endless alluvial plains in Andalusia, like a peaceful snake wandering through cultivated land, a land made particularly fertile by waters from its floods.

MURCIA

Murcia, on the banks of the River Segura, is the capital city of the Spanish province bearing the same name, where beautiful, sun-blessed coasts lie on front of fertile hills full of vine-yards, citrus fruit plantations, olive groves, with pleasant woods of almond trees here and there, protected in the background by the *Cordillera Bética* and its high peaks so romantically snow-capped for many months of the year. Founded in 825 by Abd al Rahman II, the city had the benefit of being substantially independent for many decades when it was under Arabian rule, except for the brief period of Valencia supremacy (1038-1065) and the Sevillian one later on (1078-1091). Conquered in 1243 by Ferdinand III and officially annexed to the Castile kingdom 23 years later, Murcia has preserved its antique centre, crossed through by the *Calle de la Trapería*, a pedestrian street that connects the ancient Market Square to the striking **Cathedral**, certainly the most famous and significant monument remaining in what is substantially, profoundly a Moorish city, with its patios, its decorations, its ancient whitewashed buildings. The Cathedral is antique, too, since it was started in 1394 over the principal mosque in the city, as was the custom. Consecrated to worship in 1467, an imposing *tower* was very gradually added on at different stages between the XVI and XVIII centuries. Then, between 1739 and 1754 the Baroque *façade* was added by the architect Jaime Bort, who purposely created a stunning effect of lavish grandeur. The same grandeur can be seen in the *chapels* at each side of the building: the late-Gothic *Capilla de los Vélez* built between the end of the XV century and the beginning of the XVI century, and the austere *Capilla de los Junterones*, built in the first half of the XVI century in pure Renaissance style. Next to the Cathedral, there is also a rich and interesting **Museum** where visitors can admire precious Gothic altarpieces as well as Roman relics and extremely beautiful religious items, such

as the third-largest *monstrance* in the whole of Spain. The real treasure of Murcia and its province is, however (and it can be said without appearing sacrilegious), the produce from its fertile countryside, particularly its red, white and rosé wines. In the *Jumilla* area, for instance, hot summers mature the black *Monastrell* grapes, which yield full-bodied, sweet and generally very strong, red wines. And *Yecla*, farther East, is another region famous for its top quality, wines.

Left: the XVIII façade of Murcia Cathedral. Above and insert: the real 'gold' of the region, its wine, made from local grapes grown in luxuriant vineyards.

One of the most beautiful spots in Valencia, Plaza de la Virgen, from where the sober, imposing Cathedral can be admired.

VALENCIA

Standing in the centre of a coastal plain transformed into citrus-fruit plantations with the aid of skilful irrigation, Valencia, the third largest city in Spain, was once a prosperous Roman colony on the banks of the River Guadalquivir, and was populated in 138 BC by Viriatus veterans sent by Decimus Junius Brutus. Occupied by the Visigoths in 413 and conquered by the Moors in 714, from 1031 to 1094 it was the capital of a kingdom that took its name. Ruled by El Cid, and then by his widow Ximena (1094-1102), before being taken over once more by the Arabs, Valencia was finally annexed to the Aragona kingdom in 1238 by Jaime I, the Conqueror. From then on, Christians and Moors lived side by side, peacefully and profitably, and the city went through a long period of prosperity right up until the War of the Spanish Succession, when it unfortunately decided to take side with Charles of Hapsburg, the Archduke of Austria. Today, Valencia is a thriving, animated city, full of businesses, cultural centres, museums, institutions, and is famous for its warm climate and the passionate temperament of its people, who all turn out in March for *Las Fallas*, one of the most spectacular Spanish *Fiestas* during which enormous papier-mâché statues are burned and a carpet of flowers is prepared to honour the sacred image of the Patron of the city, the *Virgen de los Desamparados*, the 'Madonna of the Abandoned'. There is also a basilica dedicated to the Virgin Mother but the most important church in Valencia is undoubtedly the **Cathedral**, started in 1262 and extended and reconstructed so many times that the three doorways are all different in style: the Romanesque *Puerta del Palau*, the oldest of the three, the Gothic *Puerta de los Apóstoles,* and the Baroque *Puerta de los Hierros*. Cherished inside the Cathedral is what legends believe to be the *Holy Grail*, an agate goblet supposed to have been brought here from Jerusalem; standing 68 metres high beside the building is its imposing octagonal *bell-tower,* symbol of the city, built between 1380 and 1420, and more familiarly called the *Miguelete*. But Valencia has yet another famous doorway, the **Torres de Serranos**, a sort of triumphal archway built into the city walls in 1238 and featuring two magnificent battlemented towers, embellished with unusual, elegant Gothic fretwork.

One of the original figures that stand out on the façade of the Museo Nacional de Céramica, one of the most famous historical-cultural institutions in Valencia.

A view of Plaza del Ayuntamiento, and bottom left, a glimpse of the typical futuristic constructions in the Ciudad de las Artes y las Ciencias.

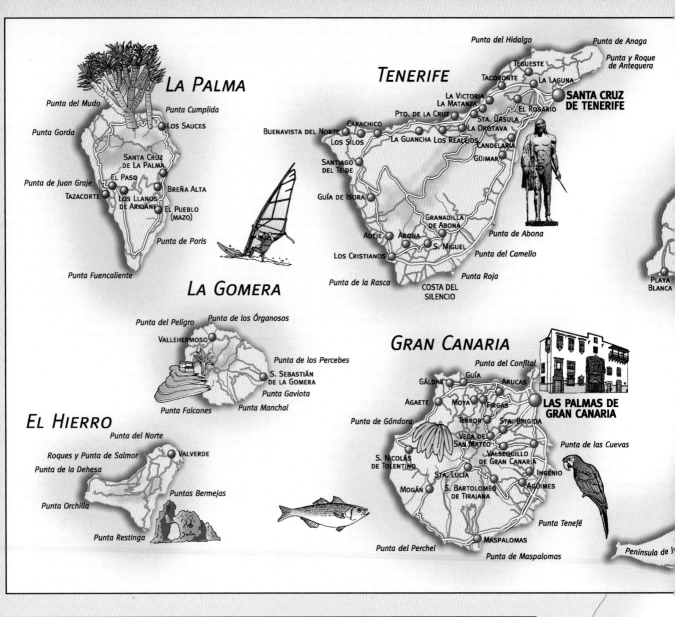

LA PALMA

Punta del Mudo
Punta Cumplida
Punta Gorda
Los Sauces
Punta de Juan Graje
Santa Cruz de La Palma
El Paso
Breña Alta
Tazacorte
Los Llanos de Aridane
El Pueblo (Mazo)
Punta de Poris
Punta Fuencaliente

TENERIFE

Punta del Hidalgo
Punta de Anaga
Punta y Roque de Antequera
Tegueste
Tacoronte
La Laguna
SANTA CRUZ DE TENERIFE
La Victoria
La Matanza
El Rosario
Pto. de la Cruz
Sta. Úrsula
La Orotava
Carachico
Buenavista del Norte
La Guancha Los Realejos
Candelaria
Los Silos
Güimar
Santiago del Teide
Guía de Isora
Granadilla de Abona
Punta de Abona
Adeje
Arona
Punta del Camello
S. Miguel
Los Cristianos
Punta Roja
Punta de la Rasca
COSTA DEL SILENCIO
PLAYA BLANCA

LA GOMERA

Punta del Peligro
Punta de los Órganosos
Vallehermoso
Punta de los Percebes
S. Sebastián de la Gomera
Punta Gaviota
Punta Falcones
Punta Manchal

GRAN CANARIA

Punta del Confital
Guía
Gáldar
Arucas
Agaete
Moya
Firgas
LAS PALMAS DE GRAN CANARIA
Terror
Sta. Brígida
Punta de Góndora
Vega de San Mateo
Punta de las Cuevas
Valsequillo de Gran Canaria
S. Nicolás de Tolentino
Ingenio
Sta. Lucía
Agüimes
Mogán
S. Bartolomé de Tirajana
Punta Tenefé
Punta del Perchel
MASPALOMAS
Punta de Maspalomas
Península de \

EL HIERRO

Punta del Norte
Roques y Punta de Salmor
VALVERDE
Punta de la Dehesa
Puntas Bermejas
Punta Orchilla
Punta Restinga

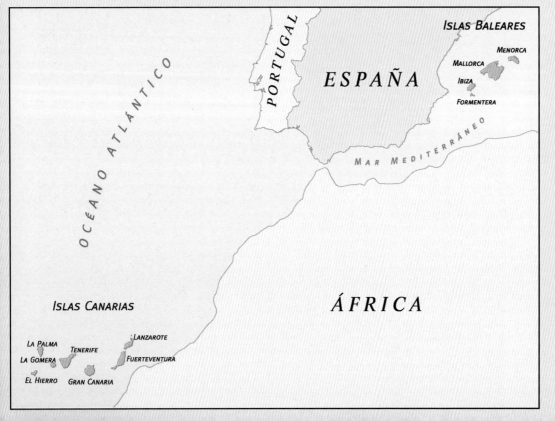

PORTUGAL

ISLAS BALEARES

MENORCA

MALLORCA

ESPAÑA

IBIZA

FORMENTERA

O C É A N O   A T L Á N T I C O

MAR MEDITERRÁNEO

ISLAS CANARIAS

ÁFRICA

LA PALMA
LANZAROTE
TENERIFE
LA GOMERA
FUERTEVENTURA
EL HIERRO   GRAN CANARIA

RARE PEARLS IN THE SEAS

Many parts of Spain, the largest country in an extensive peninsula, face onto the sea: on the East, the warm waters of the
Mediterranean Sea, to the West, beyond the Strait of Gibraltar,
the colder waters of the Atlantic Ocean, then from Galicia and
along the northern coast the country looks over the deep waters of the vast Bay of Biscay. In effect, Spanish history owes
much to these vast coastlines since the sea has always played a
leading role in the country's discoveries, victories, colonisation
of other lands, and immense treasures. Different jewels, though
just as precious, still sparkle in the Spanish seas: these are the
two large archipelagos that have been rightfully annexed to the
realm; those splendid, flourishing islands covered with lush
vegetation, where fertile mountains and crystal-clear seas are
blessed by the sun, where both are a paradise for tourism yet
steeped in traces of ancient civilisations. Off one coast, the
Balearic Islands with their microcosm of white-washed houses
and prehistoric monuments emerging from the peaceful waters
of the Mediterranean Sea, and off
the other, scattered along
the African coast in
the Atlantic Ocean,
the volcanic Ca-
nary Islands
with their spec-
tacular beach-
es and fa-
mous nature
parks.

ISLA DE
ALEGRANZA

MONTAÑA CLARA

GRACIOSA

TEGUISE

OMÉ

ARRECIFE

LANZAROTE

CORRALEJO

LA OLIVA

TINDAYA

PUERTO DEL ROSARIO

BETANCURIA

PÁJARA

TUINEJE

UERTEVENTURA

CIUTADELLA

ES MERCADAL

ALAYOR

MAÓ

ES CASTELL
VILLACARLOS

MENORCA

POLLENÇA

ALCÚDIA

SA POBLA

SÓLLER

VALLDEMOSSA

INCA

MURO

ALFÀBIA

ARTÀ

CAPDEPERA

MALLORCA

MARRATXÍ

STA. MARGALIDA

SON SEVERA

ANDRATX

**PALMA DE
MALLORCA**

PETRA

SA CABANETA

MANACOR

COVES DEL DRAC

CALVIÀ

LLUCMAYOR

FELANITX

CAMPOS
DEL PORT

SANTANYÍ

IBIZA

PORTINATX

Cap d'Aubarca

SANT ANTONI ABAT

ILLA DES BOSC

SANT JOSEP

SANTA EULÀRIA
DES RIU

EIVISSA
(IBIZA)

ESPALMADOR

ESPARDELL

Punta des Borronar

Punta de Sa Pedrera

FORMENTERA

SANT FRANCESC
DE FORMENTERA
Punta Rasa

Punta de Sa Creu

Punta Rotja

Cap de Barbària

CABRERA

IR 107

N

Above: the magnificent Gothic Cathedral among the greenery of Palma de Majorca. Left: Valldemossa, famous for its impressive, large Charterhouse.

THE BALEARIC ISLANDS

Four islands surrounded by a scattering of tiny deserted isles, all emerging from the waters in the Northwest corner of the Mediterranean Sea: these are the Balearic Islands, for centuries the farthermost defence posts protecting the Spanish coasts and also, during more peaceful moments in history, indispensable halts for trade ships sailing towards northern Europe. Man settled here in the fifth millennium BC, allured by the advantageous position, the fertile soil and the beauty of the land. At around 1500-1000 BC, the so-called 'Talaiots Civilisation' emerged (the name comes from the typical stone, tower-shaped constructions, probably dwellings, which are found all around the second largest of the islands, Minorca): this was a population of civilised navigators who were probably natives of eastern Mediterranean lands. Thereafter, Phoenicians and Greeks arrived, then Carthaginians, who developed the use of catapults as weapons on the islands (hence, the Greek term used to describe the islands: *Balear Maior* and *Balear Minor*, resulting in Majorca and Minorca). Then the Romans came along and conquered the archipelago in 121 BC, followed by the Vandals in 426 AD, and the Arabs in 848. It was when the islands were annexed to the powerful Cordoba Emirate that the architecture was influenced, and the typical small white houses seen everywhere descend from this Andalusian style. The dialect spoken on the islands is clearly of Catalan origin: this traces back to the settlers who came here after James I of Aragona conquered the Balearic Islands in 1229. From that moment on, the archipelago continued its incessant progress towards economical,

Golf

When thinking of the Balearic Islands, one automatically imagines the sea, the sun, beaches, inlets and promontories, giving very little thought to the green plains that are typical in the inland areas of the islands, particularly in Majorca. However, these areas have been groomed into beautiful stretches of grass and lawns to host a sport that has become extremely popular over recent decades: golf. One more reason for enticing tourists already attracted to the archipelago.

Views of some of the most beautiful and least contaminated parts of Majorca: from top to bottom, Cala Figuera, Cala Guya and the sun-kissed beach of Alcudía.

cultural and artistic prosperity – even if the many watchtowers scattered around the islands tell of the age-long fear of attacks from pirates. Today, **Majorca**, which is the largest island, is a very popular holiday resort for tourists and has been made particularly desirable since the latter half of the XX century. Even in the XIX century, its sun-drenched inlets, the fertile plains in its countryside and the wild splendour of its hills were capable of bewitching the hearts of many artists, such as Frederick Chopin and Georges Sand who stayed here in the peaceful *Vall-demossa Charterhouse*. The most precious jewel of the archipelago stands in its capital, **Palma**, and is a wondrous spectacle for those coming in to the antique port from the sea: the beautiful Gothic Cathedral. Its construction began in the XIII century in what was already a densely populated Arabian city, but it was finished only in 1601, when the doorway was completed. The *bell-tower* was erected in 1389, then the great *rose-window* was added 20 years later (but its stained-glass traces back to the XVI century), followed 60 years later by the *Capella de la Trinitat*, where James II and James III, both of Aragona, are buried. The interior, which has one of the widest *naves* in the world (almost 20 metres wide), was reconstructed at the beginning of the XX century by Antoni Gaudí, who also designed the wrought-iron *canopy*. However, everything in Palma is flavoured with splendour and charm,

The ancient fortified citadel dominating the port of Ibiza, where local traditions – and the folk dancing that fascinates tourists – still keep their charm.

from its spectacular buildings to its sumptuous churches and its tiny, fascinating streets. This charm pervades the other towns in the island as well, from *Andratx* to *Sóller,* and *Deiá;* an island that has managed to keep large areas of its coasts and countryside from being contaminated, in spite of the obvious benefit tourism brings it.

Even less contaminated is the green island of Minorca, the one farthest from the continent and under the British flag until almost the end of the XVIII century; this island is rich in pre-historical settlements and historical sites, like the picturesque *Maó* and *Ciutadella* and other beautiful monuments. However, the island that has attracted and benefited most from tourism is the one nearest the Spanish coast, **Ibiza,** which today is a real paradise for those looking for fun, and especially night life: hotels, fashionable restaurants, huge discos, bars and all sorts of places enliven the days

and particularly the nights on the island, from the capital town bearing the same name, an ancient citadel dominated by majestic monuments (the *Punic necropolis* at *Puig des Molins,* the Gothic *Cathedral,* the fortified walls, the Baroque *Església de Santo Domingo*) to popular *Sant Antoni,* teeming with tourists, *Sant Josep* with its nearby great salt lakes called *Ses Salines,* nowadays a sanctuary for many types of birds, including flamingos, but for many centuries one of the principal resources in the archipelago since enormous quantities of salt were exported from here to Spain and the rest of Europe. In spite of its fame as a resort among all classes of tourists, including the international jet set, Ibiza has still managed to preserve some parts as nature oases and uncontaminated countryside, especially towards the northern side of the island where the fertile countryside is green with olive groves and woods where fig trees and almond trees grow in abundance. Nearby is **Formentera**, the smallest of the Balearic Islands, the wildest and most deserted, the one that has been even more successful regards avoiding contamination. The island is completely flat, except for the headland where there is a XVIII lighthouse, and there are few inhabited centres (*Sa Savina*, the little harbour where the boats berth, and *Sant Francesc*, the chief town); a panorama of the many little coves and deserted beaches, like *Illetas*, *Llevant* and *Mitjorn*, can be admired from the small plateau called *La Mola*. Very few buses drive along the winding roads, but the best way to see Formentera is definitely to hire a bicycle or a moped and venture around it like modern explorers.

Some of the most delightful features of the Balearic Islands: above and above left, a romantic little church on Ibiza and an example of the typical Formentera craftsmanship; left, a row of bicycles, a very common scene in the smallest island in the archipelago.

THE CANARY ISLANDS

Seven islands, six little isles, four national parks, hundreds of volcanoes, nearly all of which are now inactive: this is a brief outline of an archipelago that lies off the West coast of Morocco, near the Tropic of Cancer. Annexed to Spain between the XIV and XV centuries when the earliest inhabitants, the Guanches, were still there, then transformed into a flourishing trading centre on the shipping and trade routes to the American and African continents, these

Views of Tenerife: clockwise from the top, the imposing outline of the Teide mountain dominating the island; one of the gigantic statues of the Guanches seen along the Candelaria shore; and an example of the characteristic volcanic rock 'sculptures' seen inland.

islands are nowadays two distinct Spanish provinces: the Western Islands (Tenerife, La Palma, El Hierro and La Gomera) and the Eastern Islands (Gran Canaria, Lanzarote, Fuerteventura). The fantastic scenery, pleasant climate and beautiful sea have all made this place a paradise for tourism, though tourists seem to prefer the easternmost islands; **La Palma**, **El Hierro** and **La Gomera** are practically still free of important resorts. **Tenerife** is the most popular; its name derives from the Guanches dialect name for 'Snow-clad Mountain', clearly referring to the imposing *Pico del Teide*, which is the 3718 metre high inactive volcano that dominates this triangular island and is the highest in the whole of Spain. Besides seeing the capital of Tenerife, *Santa Cruz*, with its white beaches, its churches and interesting museums, the great *Parque Nacional del Teide* is definitely worth a visit: the park stretches for kilometres in the barren, lavic scenery that skirts the two volcano cones of the mountain, interrupted only here and there by defiant but rare and beautiful and plants.

The situation in the Eastern Islands is somewhat different. Particularly in **Gran Canaria**, which attracts almost two million tourists every year; besides a microcosm of scenery and climate (sandy coasts and cliffs, beaches and green countryside, rugged peaks and valleys at the foot of the great volcano cone in the centre of the island), the island

A beautiful panoramic view of the city of Las Palmas, modern yet rich in outstanding monuments and relics of its ancient splendour.

has two very famous cities, **Las Palmas** and Maspalomas. The former is the chief city and the largest in the province, with a very busy port where modern facilities flank the ancient architecture of the old district. Hence, next to the XVI *Cathedral* consecrated to *Santa Ana*, and the *Casa de Colón*, the government building that accommodated Christopher Columbus and now a museum dedicated to his adventures, visitors can see the picturesque *Pueblo Canario*, a tourist paradise of little whitewashed houses, where the sounds of folk music and dancing fill the air around busy little shops selling the ware of local craftsmen. Then there is the *Museo Canario*, entirely dedicated to the rich, interesting history of the Canary Islands prior to the arrival of the Spaniards; and the *Parque Santa Catalina*, a shaded square facing the port and full of typical kiosks and delightful meeting places.
In **Maspalomas**, the atmosphere is different: a host of hotels, restaurants, holiday *bungalows*, nightclubs, a popular *casinò*, sandy beaches and reefs, golf courses and swimming pools.
Everything here means tourism, even for the elite, from *San Agustín*, the easternmost district, to *Playa del Inglés*, the heart of the tourist resort. And not far away lies one of Nature's masterpieces: the famous *Dunas de Mas-*

Opposite page: top, the rocky peaks of the massif that soars in the centre of Gran Canaria offer a spectacular sight as they emerge from their perpetual cloak of clouds; below, the windswept dunes in Maspalomas, a famous scene reminiscent of Africa.

palomas, a spectacular nature reserve with vast sandy dunes continuously remodelled and redistributed by the winds.

However, **Lanzarote** is where the scenery plays the uppermost role, mainly because strict regulations (severe limitations regards the height, size and colour of the buildings) have restricted the development of mass tourism so as to avoid altering the wild appearance of the easternmost of the Canary Islands.

Of volcanic origin, demonstrated by the dark lavic soil, mainly barren because of the chronic lack of

Sparse vegetation, vast sun-baked areas, white-washed houses and peasants riding their donkeys: this is the peaceful atmosphere offered in the heart of Lanzarote.

Excursions on dromedaries along the slopes of dark lava rock, ancient volcanoes lying asleep but not dead, windmills capturing the energy of the winds that blow incessantly here, delightful beaches coasting the crystal-clear sea: everyday scenes in this island in the Canary archipelago.

water, with white beaches, a scattering of fishing villages, windmills and turbines exploiting the energy of the winds that blow practically all the time in this sunny place, Lanzarote has been carefully protected and is a truly pleasant island for savouring tourism still on a human scale. While most of the tourists holiday in *Playa Blanca*, *Puerto del Carmen*, *Arrecife* or *Costa Teguise*, none can resist the classical excursion inland towards the volcanic heart of the island, to the *Parque Nacional de Timanfaya* where the terrible eruptions of the *Montañas de Fuego* have covered the barren land throughout the ages with a blanket of lava, ashes and lapilli. Hot springs and flame-spurting cracks in the rocks demonstrate that the volcano in Lanzarote is sleeping, but not dead. Not like in the period between 1730 and 1736, when the devastating eruptions showered disaster on the island and many, many villages were destroyed. All that can be seen now of the violence of those tragic moments are the awesome stretches of lava flow where it is difficult to get anything to grow, in spite of the fact that there is still a considerable amount of agriculture in Lanzarote, and in the other parts of the Canary Islands, for that matter; and country folk riding up and down the steep, winding lanes on their donkeys is not a rare sight. On the other hand, a unique experience for tourists is to ride on dromedaries, the tough agile animals that can climb the steep slopes of lava effortlessly.

Another practically barren island is **Fuerteventura**, the biggest in the Eastern Islands, and the least populated one, too, where the goats that incessantly chew the poor vegetation outnumber the just over 30,000 inhabitants. Actually, several centuries ago this island was covered with thick forests, but the Spanish colonisers systematically felled the trees for timber. Since then, and because the winds blow relentlessly over the land, the climate in Fuerteventura has become arid and dry, the flora has become just shrub-like and sporadic, and water is so scarce that it has to be shipped here in tankers for everyday use.

Again, however, the wealth of the island lies in tourism, though this has yet to be fully established. Nevertheless, those who have visited the island have been absolutely enthralled by the beauty of the isolated beaches, the wonderful scenery offered by the volcanic peaks inland, by the fascinating little villages of *Betancuria* and *Pájara*, and by the easy-going, relaxing atmosphere of life on the island.

Deserted sandy shores face the cobalt-blue sea and contribute to the captivating allure of Fuerteventura, an island with much to be discovered.

Flowers in the Canary Islands

The Lavatera acerifolia, commonly called wild mallow, is one of the endemic shrubs of the Canary Islands and its large flowers are hued the typical mauve that becomes darker, however, towards the base of the petals. It can reach 2.5 metres in height and grow even in very arid environments.

Originally from South-East Asia, the Alpinia zerumbet is a herbaceous, rhizomatous plant that can grow to even 3.5 metres high and its leaves can measure up to 75 centimetres in length. It is particularly appreciated in floriculture because of its spectacular blooms and the fact that it flowers all year round.

A plant typically found in rocky environments, the Antirrhinum majus or snapdragon grows in many places in the world, not only in the Canary Islands where it can be seen amongst the rocks hot from the sun or even growing on stone walls. There are many varieties and these often differ only in the colour of their flowers, always very bright in range from yellow to white with purple streaks, or even dark purple.

The stony borders of the roads in the Canary Islands are often brightened with the vividly coloured Tropaeolum majus, nasturtiums with their yellow, orange and dark red flowers. Originally from South America (Columbia, Peru, Bolivia) and introduced during the second half of the XVII century to Europe where it now grows profusely, the whole plant is edible and even an oil is extracted from it.

INDEX

Publication created and designed by Casa Editrice Bonechi
Editorial management: Giovanna Magi
Graphic design, layout and cover: Sonia Gottardo
Picture research: Francesco Giannoni and Sonia Gottardo
Make up: Federica Balloni
Editing: Patrizia Fabbri
Text: Patrizia Fabbri
Translation: Shona Cunningham Dryburgh
Illustrations: Stefano Benini

© Copyright by Casa Editrice Bonechi - Firenze - Italia
E-mail: bonechi@bonechi.it - Internet: www.bonechi.it - www.bonechi.com

Printed in Italy by Centro Stampa Editoriale Bonechi.

The majority of the photographs are property of the Casa Editrice Bonechi Archives. They were taken by Marco Bonechi, Serena de Leonardis, Luigi Di Giovine, Andrea Fantauzzo, Paolo Giambone, Andrea Innocenti, Andrea Pistolesi, Antonio Quattrone, Alessandro Saragosa.
Other photographs were provided by
Spanish Embassy in Italy (by kind permission): page 7; Gianni Dagli Orti: pages 6 left, 35 above, 40 below, 46 above, 52, 53, 56-57 below, 64 above left, 78 below, 114-115, 122, 123, 134 below; Maurizio Fraschetti: pages 44-45, 50-51, 56-57 above, 60-61, 66-67, 90-91, 126, 174-175, 175 below; Sonia Gottardo: (by kind permission) pages 16 below right and 17 right above and below; 27 below and 190; Heeresgeschichtliches Museum, Vienna: page 34 below; Prado Museum: pages 5 above, 94, 95, 96, 97; OTUS: page 5 below; Photos Patrimonio Nacional: page 101 (three bottom photographs); Lara Pessina: page 174 below; Andrea Pistolesi: pages 16 (except the photographs below right and above left), 16-17, 30 above, 38, 39, 138, 139, 164-165; Ghigo Roli: pages 54, 55 above, 124-125, 148, 149, 152, 153, 158, 162, 163, 172-173; Scala Group: pages 3, 6 right; Nico Tondini, Focus Team, Milan: pages 154-155; Spanish Tourist Board Office, Rome (by kind permission): page 160 above and below right (López Alonso), page 160 below left (Juan J. Pascal), pages 176, 177 below right and left; Sandro Vannini: page 31 below right and left.

The Publisher gratefully acknowledges the Spanish Embassy in Italy and the Spanish Tourist Board Office in Rome for their valuable collaboration.

ISBN 88-476-0833-3

* * *